INTELLECTUAL PROPERTY IN THE 21ST CENTURY

INTELLECTUAL PROPERTY RIGHTS

BACKGROUND, INTERNATIONAL TRADE PROTECTION AND THE ROLE OF EXCLUSION ORDERS

INTELLECTUAL PROPERTY IN THE 21ST CENTURY

Additional books in this series can be found on Nova's website under the Series tab.

Additional e-books in this series can be found on Nova's website under the e-book tab.

INTELLECTUAL PROPERTY IN THE 21ST CENTURY

INTELLECTUAL PROPERTY RIGHTS

BACKGROUND, INTERNATIONAL TRADE PROTECTION AND THE ROLE OF EXCLUSION ORDERS

EVELYN P. GILBERT
EDITOR

nova publishers
New York

Library of Congress Cataloging-in-Publication Data

ISBN: 978-1-63482-396-8

Published by Nova Science Publishers, Inc. † New York

Contents

PREFACE

Intellectual property rights (IPR) are legal rights granted by governments to encourage innovation and creative output by ensuring that creators reap the benefits of their inventions or works. They may take forms such as patents, trade secrets, copyrights, trademarks, or geographical indications. Congress has constitutional responsibility for legislating and overseeing IPR and international trade policy. Responsibility for developing IPR policy, engaging in IPR-related international negotiations, and enforcing IPR laws cuts across multiple U.S. government agencies. This book provides background on IPR and discusses the role of U.S. international trade policy in enhancing IPR protection and enforcement abroad. This book also describes Customs and Border Protection's (CBP) processes for enforcing exclusion orders; and assesses CBP's management of its enforcement process at ports of entry.

Chapter 1 – This report provides background on intellectual property rights (IPR) and discusses the role of U.S. international trade policy in enhancing IPR protection and enforcement abroad. IPR are legal rights granted by governments to encourage innovation and creative output by ensuring that creators reap the benefits of their inventions or works. They may take forms such as patents, trade secrets, copyrights, trademarks, or geographical indications. Congress has constitutional responsibility for legislating and overseeing IPR and international trade policy. Responsibility for developing IPR policy, engaging in IPR-related international negotiations, and enforcing IPR laws cuts across multiple U.S. government agencies. The protection and enforcement of IPR is an important and longstanding component of U.S. international trade policy and U.S. trade negotiating objectives. U.S. trade policy also seeks to address new and evolving issues in the IPR landscape related to the growing role of emerging markets in the global market place and the increased level of digital trade. Since the North American Free Trade Agreement (NAFTA) and the 1995 Agreement on Trade-Related Aspects of Intellectual Property Rights (TRIPS Agreement) at the World Trade Organization (WTO), trade policy has been used to advance IPR rules internationally. The TRIPS Agreement set minimum standards for IPR protection and enforcement. The United States engages in efforts with other trading partners to build on the TRIPS Agreement, particularly through the negotiation of regional and bilateral free trade agreements (FTAs). To date, the United States has entered into 14 FTAs with 20 countries, which generally include IPR commitments exceeding obligations under the TRIPS Agreement. The May 10, 2007, bipartisan trade agreement modified some of the IPR requirements in the U.S. FTAs with Peru, Panama and Colombia, allowing for greater flexibility for these developing countries to meet both their IPR obligations and public health needs. IPR issues are prominent in the ongoing U.S. FTA negotiations of the proposed Trans-Pacific Partnership (TPP) and Transatlantic Trade and Investment Partnership (TTIP). The United States also seeks to build on the TRIPS Agreement in other ways, such as through the negotiation of the Anti-Counterfeiting Trade Agreement (ACTA). Other trade policy tools also are available to advance U.S. international IPR objectives. Pursuant to Section 182 of the Trade Act of 1974 as amended (P.L. 93-618), the Office of the U.S. Trade Representative (USTR) identifies countries providing inadequate IPR protection in its annual "Special 301" report. Section 337 of the amended Tariff Act of 1930 authorizes the U.S. International Trade Commission (ITC) to prohibit U.S. imports that infringe on U.S. IPR. Additionally, under the Generalized System of Preferences (GSP), the United States may consider a developing country's IPR policies and practices as a basis for offering or suspending preferential duty-free entry to certain products from the country. IPR issues related to international trade policy may figure prominently in congressional agenda. Congress may: examine the role of IPR in U.S. trade policy, including through consideration of IPR trade negotiating objectives in a renewal of Trade Promotion Authority (TPA); conduct oversight of implementation of the IPR commitments in existing trade agreements, as well as in the current U.S. trade negotiations on the TPP and TTIP; conduct oversight of the role of IPR in U.S. economic growth and innovation, and how the protection and enforcement of IPR relates to other public policy goals, such as access to medicines in poor or developing countries and the free flow of data; consider the possibility of additional policy options to address IPR concerns in emerging economies that are not a part of existing U.S. FTAs or included in current U.S. FTA negotiations, as well as new and evolving IPR issues, such as with respect to indigenous innovation, "forced" localization barriers to trade, and trade secret theft through cybercrime; and examine the effectiveness of the current U.S. coordinating structure and the adequacy of current federal resources for promoting international IPR support.

Chapter 2 – Under Section 337 of the Tariff Act of 1930, ITC investigates allegations of unfair import practices, including unlicensed use of intellectual property rights such as patents, copyrights, and trademarks. If ITC finds a violation of this law, it generally issues an exclusion order that directs CBP to deny entry of infringing products into U.S. commerce. CBP must determine, without inhibiting legitimate trade, whether products arriving at 328 U.S. ports are covered by exclusion orders. GAO was asked to review CBP's enforcement of exclusion orders. This report (1) describes CBP's processes for enforcing exclusion orders and (2) assesses CBP's management of its enforcement process at ports of entry. GAO analyzed CBP and ITC documents and data from October 2009 through April 2014 and interviewed CBP and ITC officials.

In: Intellectual Property Rights
Editor: Evelyn P. Gilbert
ISBN: 978-1-63482-396-8

Chapter 1

INTELLECTUAL PROPERTY RIGHTS AND INTERNATIONAL TRADE*

Shayerah Ilias Akhtar and Ian F. Fergusson

SUMMARY

This report provides background on intellectual property rights (IPR) and discusses the role of U.S. international trade policy in enhancing IPR protection and enforcement abroad. IPR are legal rights granted by governments to encourage innovation and creative output by ensuring that creators reap the benefits of their inventions or works. They may take forms such as patents, trade secrets, copyrights, trademarks, or geographical indications. Congress has constitutional responsibility for legislating and overseeing IPR and international trade policy. Responsibility for developing IPR policy, engaging in IPR-related international negotiations, and enforcing IPR laws cuts across multiple U.S. government agencies.

The protection and enforcement of IPR is an important and longstanding component of U.S. international trade policy and U.S. trade negotiating objectives. U.S. trade policy also seeks to address new and evolving issues in the IPR landscape related to the growing role of emerging markets in the global market place and the increased level of digital trade.

* This is an edited, reformatted and augmented version of a Congressional Research Service publication, No. RL34292, dated April 4, 2014.

Since the North American Free Trade Agreement (NAFTA) and the 1995 Agreement on Trade-Related Aspects of Intellectual Property Rights (TRIPS Agreement) at the World Trade Organization (WTO), trade policy has been used to advance IPR rules internationally. The TRIPS Agreement set minimum standards for IPR protection and enforcement. The United States engages in efforts with other trading partners to build on the TRIPS Agreement, particularly through the negotiation of regional and bilateral free trade agreements (FTAs). To date, the United States has entered into 14 FTAs with 20 countries, which generally include IPR commitments exceeding obligations under the TRIPS Agreement. The May 10, 2007, bipartisan trade agreement modified some of the IPR requirements in the U.S. FTAs with Peru, Panama and Colombia, allowing for greater flexibility for these developing countries to meet both their IPR obligations and public health needs. IPR issues are prominent in the ongoing U.S. FTA negotiations of the proposed Trans-Pacific Partnership (TPP) and Transatlantic Trade and Investment Partnership (TTIP). The United States also seeks to build on the TRIPS Agreement in other ways, such as through the negotiation of the Anti-Counterfeiting Trade Agreement (ACTA).

Other trade policy tools also are available to advance U.S. international IPR objectives. Pursuant to Section 182 of the Trade Act of 1974 as amended (P.L. 93-618), the Office of the U.S. Trade Representative (USTR) identifies countries providing inadequate IPR protection in its annual "Special 301" report. Section 337 of the amended Tariff Act of 1930 authorizes the U.S. International Trade Commission (ITC) to prohibit U.S. imports that infringe on U.S. IPR. Additionally, under the Generalized System of Preferences (GSP), the United States may consider a developing country's IPR policies and practices as a basis for offering or suspending preferential duty-free entry to certain products from the country.

IPR issues related to international trade policy may figure prominently in congressional agenda. Congress may:

- examine the role of IPR in U.S. trade policy, including through consideration of IPR trade negotiating objectives in a renewal of Trade Promotion Authority (TPA);
- conduct oversight of implementation of the IPR commitments in existing trade agreements, as well as in the current U.S. trade negotiations on the TPP and TTIP;
- conduct oversight of the role of IPR in U.S. economic growth and innovation, and how the protection and enforcement of IPR relates to other public policy goals, such as access to medicines in poor or developing countries and the free flow of data;

- consider the possibility of additional policy options to address IPR concerns in emerging economies that are not a part of existing U.S. FTAs or included in current U.S. FTA negotiations, as well as new and evolving IPR issues, such as with respect to indigenous innovation, "forced" localization barriers to trade, and trade secret theft through cybercrime; and
- examine the effectiveness of the current U.S. coordinating structure and the adequacy of current federal resources for promoting international IPR support.

INTRODUCTION

Intellectual property rights (IPR) traditionally have been matters of national concern. Individual nation states have developed IPR regimes reflecting their domestic needs and priorities. Over time, intellectual property protection and enforcement have come to the forefront as a key international trade issue for the United States—largely due to the importance of intellectual property as an prominent feature of an innovative U.S. economy—figuring prominently in the multilateral trade policy arena and in regional and bilateral U.S. free trade agreements (FTAs).

Congress has legislative, oversight, and appropriations responsibilities related to IPR and trade policy. The role of Congress in addressing IPR and trade-related issues stems from the U.S. Constitution, which provides Congress with the power "To promote the Progress of Science and useful Arts, by securing for limited Times to Authors and Inventors the exclusive Right to their respective Writings and Discoveries" and "To regulate Commerce with foreign Nations."[1] Congressional interest has grown in the role of IPR in advancing U.S. industrial competitiveness and contributing to U.S. economic recovery following the recent international financial crisis. Some Members of Congress also have expressed concern about U.S. economic losses associated with IPR infringement; the potential health and safety consequences of counterfeit pharmaceutical drugs and other products; the national security implications of the theft of trade secrets, including through cybercrime; and connections between organized crime and IPR infringement.

This report discusses the different kinds of IPR and forms of IPR infringement; the role of IPR in the U.S. economy; estimated losses associated with IPR infringement; the organizational structure of IPR protection in multilateral, regional, bilateral arenas; U.S. government agencies involved with IPR and trade; and issues for Congress regarding IPR and international trade.

INTELLECTUAL PROPERTY RIGHTS BASICS

This section provides definitions of various kinds of intellectual property rights (patents, trade secrets, copyrights, trademarks, and geographical indications) and intellectual property rights misappropriation (infringement, piracy, and counterfeiting).

Types of IPR

IPR are legal rights granted by governments to encourage innovation and creative output. They ensure that creators reap the benefits of their inventions or works and may take forms such as patents, trade secrets, copyrights, trademarks, or geographical indications. Through IPR, governments grant a temporary legal monopoly to innovators by giving them the right to limit or control the use of their creations by others. IPR may be traded or licensed to others, usually in return for fees and/or royalty payments. Although the World Trade Organization (WTO) Agreement on Trade-Related Aspects of Intellectual Property Rights (TRIPS) provides minimum standards for IPR protections, such rights are granted on a national basis and are, in general, enforceable only in the country in which they are granted. However, countries are obliged to abide by WTO rules, and their IPR enforcement practices can be challenged by other countries at the WTO.

Patents

The Patent Act (35 U.S.C. 101 *et seq.*) governs the issuance and use of patents in the United States. Patents are granted for inventions of new products, processes, or organisms (known as utility patents). Patents also may be granted for designs and plants. For an invention to be patentable, it must be new, "non-obvious" (involving an inventive step), and have a potential industrial or commercial application. The patent provides the holder with the exclusive right to exclude others from making, using, selling, or importing into the United States the patented invention for a period of 20 years[2] The patent right is based on the proposition that inventors must be granted a temporary monopoly over their invention in order to encourage innovation and to promote the expenditure of money on research and development (R&D). The patent holder recoups these up-front costs through a temporary monopoly over the invention. In return for this economic rent, the patent holder must disclose the content of the patent along with test data and other information concerning the invention. This is meant to spur further creativity by those seeking to build on the patent after its expiration. Domestically, patents are granted by the U.S. Patent and Trademark Office (PTO) of the Department of Commerce.

Trade Secrets

A trade secret is any type of valuable information, including a "formula, pattern, compilation, program, device, method, technique, or process," that derives independent economic value from not being generally known or readily ascertainable and is subject to reasonable efforts by the owner to maintain its secrecy.[3] Examples of trade secrets include blueprints, customer lists, pricing information, and source code. While protection of patents and copyright is an exclusive matter of federal law, trade secret protection is found not only in federal law, but also in state law. Most states have adopted the Uniform Trade Secret Act (UTSA), a model law drafted by the National Conference of Commissioners on Uniform State Laws.

There are important differences between trade secrets and patents. Individuals do not have to apply for trade secret protection as they would for patents. Protection of trade secrets originates immediately with the creation of the trade secret; there is no process for applying for protection or registering trade secrets. Trade secret protection does not expire unless the trade secret becomes known. In contrast, patent applicants must disclose information about their innovation to the PTO in order to acquire a patent. Patents offer right holders stronger protection but for a limited period of time. While applying for a patent can be a costly and lengthy process, patents are valuable if the confidentiality of the innovation is fragile or if the area of research is highly competitive.

Copyright

Protection of copyrights in the United States is based on the Copyright Act (17 U.S.C. 101, *et seq.*). Copyrights protect original expressions of authorship, fixed in physical and/or digital forms. Such protections include literary or artistic works such as books, music, sound recordings, movies, paintings, architectural works, and computer software and databases (though not individual bits of data). Traditionally, copyrights differed from patents in that there was no claim to industrial applicability or novelty of the idea. The expression of the idea, not the underlying idea, was being copyrighted. While some of the criteria for copyrights differ from those of patents, the objective is the same: investments of time, money, and effort to create work of cultural, social and economic significance should be protected to encourage further creativity. U.S. law provides copyright protection for life of the author plus 70 years for personal works, or 120 years from creation (or 95 years from publication) for corporate works. Copyrights may be registered by the U.S. Copyright Office of the Library of Congress, although protection arises immediately upon fixation in a tangible medium of expression.

Trademarks

Trademark protection in the United States is governed jointly by state and federal law. The main federal statute is the Lanham Act of 1946 (15 U.S.C. 1051, *et seq.*). Also known as service marks, trademarks permit the seller to use a distinctive name, mark, symbol, or sound to identify and market a product, service, or company. The trademark allows quick identification of the seller's product, and for good or ill, can become an indicator of a product's quality. If for good, the trademark can be valuable in the introduction of new products by conveying an instant assurance of quality. The trademark is designed to prevent other companies with similar merchandise from free-riding on the association of quality with the trademarked item. Thus, a trademarked good may command a premium in the marketplace because of its reputation. For trademarks, distinctiveness is at a premium because a trademark must capture the consumer's imagination to be effective as generic names of commodities cannot be trademarked. Trademark rights are acquired through use or through registration with the PTO.

A related concept to trademarks is the **geographic indication,** which is also protected by the Lanham Act. The geographic indication acts to protect the quality and reputation of a distinctive product originating in a certain region; however, the benefit does not accrue to a sole producer, but rather the producers of a product originating from a particular region. Geographic indications are generally sought for agricultural products, or wines and spirits. Protection for geographical indications is acquired in the United States by registration with the PTO, through a process similar to trademark registration. In general, however, the United States protects geographic indications through trademark law.

Infringement of IPR

IPR infringement is the misappropriation or violation of the IPR. In the case of patents, infringement of a patent owner's exclusive rights (as afforded by patent laws) involves a third party's unauthorized use of the patented invention. As relates to international trade, the greatest challenge to the patent right is infringement in foreign countries, or non-observance by WTO member states to the minimal standards of the TRIPS Agreement. Copyright infringement occurs when a third party engages in reproducing, performing, or distributing a copyrighted work without the consent of the copyright owner. In addition to the term infringement, other terms are used to describe certain violations of IPR.

Piracy

The term "piracy" has applications to both copyrights and trademarks. The major challenge facing copyright protection is piracy, either through physical duplication of the work, illegal dissemination of copyrighted material (such as computer software, music, or movies) over the Internet, and/or participation in commercial transactions of copyrighted materials without the consent of the copyright owner. With respect to trademarks, piracy involves the registration or use of a famous foreign trademark that is not registered in the country or is invalid because the trademark has not been used.

Counterfeiting

An imitation of a product is referred to as a "counterfeit" or a "fake." Counterfeit products are manufactured, marketed, and distributed with the appearance of being the genuine good and originating from the genuine manufacturer.[4] The purpose of counterfeit goods is to deceive consumers about their origin and nature. Counterfeiting and copying of original goods are major challenges for trademarked products. The counterfeited product can be sold for a premium because of its association with the original item, while reducing the sales of the original items. Furthermore, consumer experience with a counterfeited good of inferior quality, can damage the reputation of the trademark product. Popular examples of counterfeit products include fake fashionwear, such as Louis Vuitton bags or Rolex watches, or fake pharmaceutical products, such as popular brand-name prescription medicines.

A related issue is the imitation of labels and packaging of trademarked goods. In this situation, the imitator uses a trademark that is confusingly similar to a well-known trademark in order to benefit from the reputation of the product with which he is competing.

INNOVATION INDICATORS

According to the Organisation for Economic Co-operation and Development (OECD), innovation is the "implementation of a new or significantly improved product (good or service), or process, a new marketing method, or a new organizational method." Innovation is widely considered to be a key source of economic growth, and IPR to be a major driver of innovation. The measurement of innovation is an evolving field. Possible elements of innovation indicators include activities related to the commercialization of inventions and new technologies.[5] One such component could be global trends in patenting.[6] Trends in the total number of patent filing applications received under the Patent Cooperation Treaty (PCT), an international patent filing system administered by the World Intellectual Property Organization (WIPO), may be illustrative.

Table 1. Global Intellectual Property Filings Through the PCT, 2010-2012

Country of Origin	2010	2011	2012	2012 Share (%)	2011-2012 Growth (%)
TOTAL	164,338	182,379	194,400	100.0%	6.6%
United States	45,029	49,060	51,207	26.3%	4.4%
Japan	32,150	38,874	43,660	22.5%	12.3%
Germany	17,568	18,851	18,855	9.7%	0.0%
China	12,296	16,402	18,627	9.6%	13.6%
South Korea	9,669	10,447	11,848	6.1%	13.4%
France	7,246	7,438	7,739	4.0%	4.0%
United Kingdom	4,891	4,848	4,895	2.5%	1.0%
Switzerland	3,728	4,009	4,194	2.2%	4.6%
Netherlands	4,063	3,503	3,992	2.1%	14.0%
Sweden	3,314	3,462	3,585	1.8%	3.6%
Italy	2,658	2,695	2,836	1.5%	5.2%
Canada	2,698	2,945	2,748	1.4%	-6.7%
Finland	2,138	2,079	2,353	1.2%	13.2%
Australia	1,772	1,739	1,708	0.9%	-1.8%
Spain	1,772	1,729	1,687	0.9%	-2.4%
Others	13,346	14,298	14,466	7.4%	1.2%

Source: World Intellectual Property Organization.

Between 2010 and 2012, the number of patents filed under the PCT grew by nearly 7% (see **Table 1**), reflecting economic recovery after the international financial crisis of 2008-2009.[7] Intellectual property holdings that are protected by international agreements are highly concentrated in certain countries. The United States continues to be the source of the world's largest number of patent filing applications under the PCT, representing close to one-third of such filings in 2012. The United States, along with Germany and Japan, accounted for about 60% of all patent applications filed in 2012 under the PCT. China ranked as the fourth largest source of international patent filings under the PCT in 2012, representing about 10% of global filings. In recent years, China has had the highest growth rate in such filings, at about 14% in 2012.

ROLE OF INTELLECTUAL PROPERTY IN U.S. ECONOMY

Intellectual property generally is viewed as a longstanding strategic driver of U.S. productivity, economic growth, employment, higher wages, and exports. It also is considered a key source of U.S. comparative advantage, such as in innovation and high-technology products. Nearly every industry depends on it for its businesses. Among the industries that are dependent on patent protection are the aerospace, automotive, computer, consumer electronics, pharmaceutical, and semiconductor industries. Copyright-based industries include the software, data processing, motion picture, publishing, and recording industries. Other industries that indirectly benefit from IPR protection include retailers, traders, and transportation businesses, which support the distribution of goods and services derived from intellectual property.[8]

IP-intensive industries are considered to play a major role in the U.S. economy and international trade. What follows are some findings from a study by the U.S. Department of Commerce.[9]

- **U.S. economic impact.** In 2010, a subset of the most intellectual property-intensive industries directly supported 27.1 million jobs in the United States, or about 18.8% of total U.S. employment. They also indirectly supported 12.9 million U.S. jobs via the supply chain in other industries. In 2010, the wages of employees working in IP-intensive industries tended to be about 42% higher on average than those working in non-IP-intensive industries. These industries accounted for $5.06 trillion in value added to the U.S. economy, more than one-third of the U.S. gross domestic product (GDP).

- **U.S. trade in goods.** In 2010, IP-related merchandise exports amounted to $775 billion (two-thirds of total U.S. merchandise exports), while IP-related merchandise imports reached $1,336 billion (about 70% of total U.S. merchandise imports). Key sectors for IP-intensive merchandise trade include semiconductor and electric parts, basic chemicals, motor vehicles, pharmaceuticals and medicine, and computer and peripheral equipment.[10]
- **U.S. trade in services.** In 2007, exports of services by IP-intensive industries totaled about $90 billion (about 19% of total U.S. private services exports). Key sources of services exports included the software publishing, motion picture and video, financial services, science R&D, and management and technical consulting industries. The study does not provide information on imports of services by IP-intensive industries, though it should be noted that the United States runs an overall surplus in international trade in services.[11]

The role of IP-intensive industries in U.S. trade in services includes receipts (exports) and payments (imports) of royalties and licensing fees. Right holders may authorize the use of technologies, trademarks, and entertainment products that they own to entities in foreign countries, resulting in revenues through royalties and license fees. In 2012, U.S. receipts from cross-border trade in royalties and license fees (relating to patent, trademark, copyright, and other intangible rights) totaled $124.2 billion, up about 3.5% from 2011 receipts of $120.7 billion. At the same time, U.S. payments of royalties and license fees to foreign countries amounted to $39.9 billion, up about 5% from the 2011 level of $34.8 billion. As with overall U.S. trade in services, U.S. cross-border trade in royalties and license fees generated a trade surplus—of $84.3 billion in 2012, a small decline from $85.9 billion in 2011. U.S. trade in royalties and licenses accounted for about 16% of total U.S. trade in private services in 2012.[12]

Industry-specific figures may further demonstrate the importance of intellectual property to the U.S. economy. For example:

- **Copyright industries.** According to a study commissioned by the International Intellectual Property Alliance (IIPA), in 2012, industries categorized as part of the "core" copyright industries (e.g., computer software, videogames, books, newspapers, periodicals and journals, motion pictures, recorded music, and radio and television broadcasting) contributed about $1 trillion to the U.S. economy ("value-added" to current GDP), representing about 6.5% of the U.S. economy. The study also estimated that the "core" copyright industries employed nearly 5.4 million workers in 2012, representing about 4% of the total U.S. workforce. In addition, the study estimated that foreign sales of certain U.S. copyright sectors totaled $142 billion in 2012.[13]

- **Pharmaceutical industry.** In 2012, domestic sales by pharmaceutical companies that are members of the Pharmaceutical Researchers and Manufacturers of America (PhRMA) reached an estimated $178 billion, while sales abroad by PhRMA members totaled about $117 billion.[14]

Some advocates of civil liberties assert that empirical analysis on the role of IPR in the U.S. economy may not be fully evaluating the economic and commercial benefits of lawful exceptions and limitations to exclusive rights. For example, by one estimate, businesses that rely on "fair use" exceptions to U.S. copyright law contribute $2.2 trillion to the U.S. economy. The "fair use" doctrine provides limitations and exceptions to the exclusive rights afforded by copyright law. It permits limited use of copyrighted works without requiring permission from the right holder in certain cases, examples of which may include news reporting, research, teaching, and library use.[15]

PREVALENCE AND ECONOMIC CONSEQUENCES OF IPR INFRINGEMENT

Advances in information and technology and declining costs of transportation and communication, spurred by globalization, have fundamentally changed information and trade flows. Such changes have created new markets for U.S. exporters, but at the same time, have been associated with the proliferation of counterfeiting and piracy on a global scale.

Several factors contribute to the growing problem of IPR infringement. While the costs and time for research and development are high, IPR infringement occurs with relatively low costs and risks and a high profit margin. According to PhRMA, it takes a pharmaceutical company about 10 to 15 years of R&D to create a new drug, and the average cost to develop a drug in the early 2000s was about $1.2 billion, with costs possibly higher in more recent years. In 2012, PhRMA member companies collectively spent nearly $49 billion for research and development (domestic and abroad).[16] In contrast, drug counterfeiters can lower production costs by using inexpensive, and perhaps dangerous or ineffective, ingredient substitutes.

The development of technologies and products that can be easily duplicated, such as recorded or digital media, also has led to an increase in counterfeiting and piracy. Increasing Internet usage has contributed to the distribution of counterfeit and pirated products. Additionally, civil and criminal penalties often are not sufficient deterrents for piracy and counterfeiting. The United States is especially concerned with *foreign* IPR infringement of U.S. intellectual property. Compared to foreign countries, IPR infringements levels in the United States are considered to be relatively low.[17]

Limitations on Data Estimating IPR Infringement Costs

Quantification of the economic losses associated with IPR infringement has been a longstanding focus in the academic, policy, and industry literature. Many experts agree that it is difficult to quantify the magnitude of IPR theft with any precision. Reasons may include

- **Illicit nature of IPR infringement.** Because IPR infringement is illicit and secretive, tools that are used to measure legitimate business activity cannot necessarily be used to measure economic losses from IPR infringement. As such, it may be easier to quantify the positive contribution of copyright industries to the U.S. economy more precisely than to measure the losses to the U.S. economy from copyright piracy.
- **Quantifying specific components of economic impact.** The economic impact of IPR infringement depends on a range of factors, including the different types of infringing goods being sold, the rate at which consumers substitute buying infringing goods for legitimate goods, and IPR infringement's deterrence to R&D. It may be difficult to measure precisely these components of the economic impact of IPR infringement.[18]
- **Assumptions used to calculate economic impact.** Methods for calculating data on counterfeiting and piracy often involve certain assumptions. Estimates of losses from IPR infringement can be highly

sensitive to how these assumptions are derived and weighted. The basic economic model employed in some IPR loss estimates assumes that there is substitutability between pirated and legitimate goods. For example, under this model, sales of pirated goods may be equated to revenue losses of legitimate U.S. copyright businesses. Some analysts suggest that legitimate firms face a competition threat *only* if the individuals purchasing IPR-infringing products would be able and willing to purchase the legitimate product at the price offered when IPR infringement is not present.[19] For consumers in poor developing countries, especially, this assumption may not be tenable.

- **IPR infringement in the digital environment.** While IPR infringement in the past primarily constituted counterfeiting and piracy of physical goods (such as optical media and books), in recent years, there has been a growing amount of piracy taking place through digital mediums (such as illegal downloads of music and books over the Internet). It may be more complex to measure IPR infringement that takes place in the digital environment, and in turn, more difficult to measure the associated economic losses accurately. U.S. trade losses due to copyright infringement may be higher than reported because estimates often do not account for all forms of piracy, such as Internet piracy, which is an increasingly significant contributor to copyright piracy. One study estimates that nearly 24% of global Internet traffic infringes upon copyright.[20]
- **Sources of data.** Estimates on economic losses from IPR infringement come from a range of sources, including academic, policy, and industry sources. According to a U.S. Government Accountability Office (GAO) study, the U.S. government does not systematically collect data or analyze the impacts of counterfeiting and piracy on the U.S. economy. In many cases, the federal government relies on estimates conducted by industry groups. However, companies may be reluctant to disclose their IPR losses because of possible reputational and commercial risks, and industry associations may not always release their proprietary data sources and methods, complicating efforts to verify such estimates.[21]

International Economic Effects of IPR Infringement

While assessments of the overall global economic costs of IPR infringement are limited, available evidence indicates that the adverse economic effects of global IPR infringement stand in the hundreds of billions of dollars, and are increasing.[22] Customs data on seizures of counterfeit and pirated goods may offer some idea of the magnitudes involved in terms of impact on producers and exporters. A 2007 study by the Organisation for Economic Co-operation and Development (OECD) indirectly extrapolated available customs data on seizures to conclude that world trade in counterfeit and pirated goods may have amounted to $200 billion in 2005.[23] Updated OECD estimates suggest that trade in IPR-infringing goods may have totaled up to $250 billion in 2007. During that same time period, the share of counterfeiting and pirated goods in world trade also is estimated to have increased—from 1.85% in 2000 to 1.95% in 2007.[24]

More recently, a study commissioned by the Business Action to Stop Counterfeiting and Piracy (BASCAP), a business initiative organized by the International Chamber of Commerce, built on the OECD's work. According to the BASCAP study, for the G-20 economies, the total value of counterfeit and pirated products was an estimated $455-$650 billion in 2008, and is projected to reach $1.22-$1.77 trillion in 2015 (see **Table 2**).[25]

Table 2. Estimated International Economic Losses Due to Counterfeiting and Piracy, Selected Years (Billions of U.S. Dollars)

Category	2008	2015
Internationally traded counterfeit and pirated products	$285-$360	$770-$960
Domestically produced and consumed counterfeit and pirated products	$140-$215	$370-$570
Digitally pirated products	$30-$75	$80-$240
Total	$455-$650	$1,220-$1,770

Source: Frontier Economics, *Estimating the Global Economic and Social Impacts of Counterfeiting and Piracy*, A Report Commissioned by Business Action to Stop Counterfeiting and Piracy (BASCAP), February 2011.

Notes: BASCAP economic loss estimates are restricted to the G-20 economies.

In terms of broader economy-wide effects, the BASCAP study estimated that G-20 economies lost $125 billion every year from counterfeiting and piracy due to additional impacts on trade, foreign investment, employment, and other factors. In addition, the study estimated that G-20 economies lost about 2.5 million jobs from counterfeiting and piracy; i.e., up to 2.5 million legitimate jobs could have been created in the absence of counterfeiting and piracy.[26]

U.S. Economic Effects of IPR Infringement

While specific estimates vary, the available data suggest that U.S. economic losses from IPR infringement could be significant.

Customs Seizure Data

Data on pirated and counterfeit seizures of imports at U.S. borders shed light on the magnitude of the issue in the U.S. context (see **Figure 1**). The Department of Homeland Security (DHS) made 22,848 seizures of IPR-infringing goods in FY2012, down from 24,792 seizures in FY2011 but more than double the FY2005 level of 8,022 seizures. The general trend of the increased number of seizures over time could reflect a combination of increased DHS enforcement action and growing levels of counterfeiting and piracy. The total value of DHS seizures, as measured by the manufacturer's suggested retail price (MSRP), amounted to $1.26 billion in FY2012, up from $1.11 billion in FY2011.[27] It is worth noting that customs data may be limited in that they do not reflect digital-based IPR infringement.

Of all U.S. trading partners, China continues to account for the majority of counterfeits intercepted at the U.S. border. In FY2012, seizures of goods originating from China represented 72% of all DHS seizures and $906 million in MSRP value. Other countries that were primary sources for counterfeit and pirated goods seized included Hong Kong, India, and Singapore.[28]

A top priority for the CBP is seizing counterfeit imports that endanger the health and safety of consumers, such as counterfeit healthcare products, pharmaceutical products, and consumer electronics. The total MSRP value of IPR-related seizures of commodities that represent a potential safety and security risks was about $146 million (3,402 seizures) in FY2012, down from $196 million (4,369 seizures) in FY2011. Pharmaceutical goods were the top commodity category posing safety and security risks, accounting for more than half of such seizures by both MSRP value ($83 million) and number of seizures (2,343).[29]

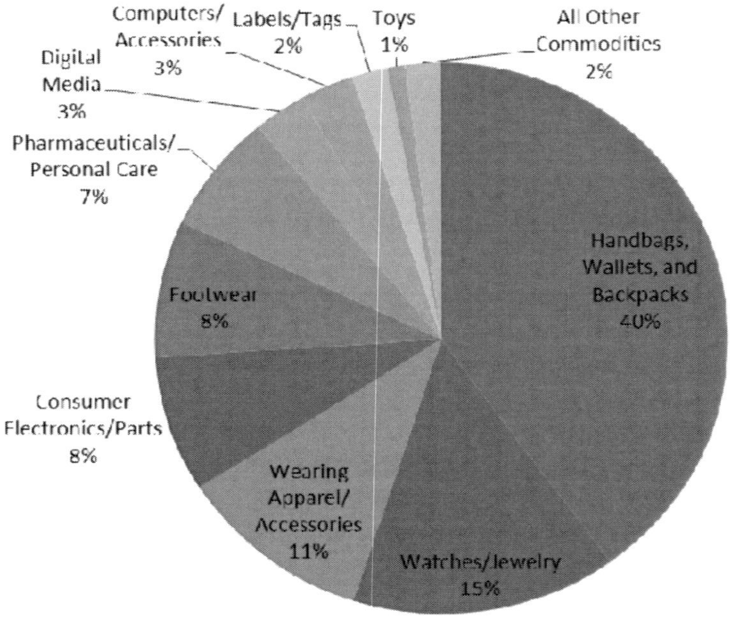

Source: Department of Homeland Security (DHS), Intellectual Property Rights: Fiscal Year 2012 Seizure Statistics.

Figure 1. Composition of U.S. Border Seizures of Counterfeit and Pirated Goods, FY2012.

Economic Loss Estimates

U.S. industries that rely on IPR protection claim to lose billions of dollars in revenue annually due to piracy and counterfeiting. Beyond these direct losses, the United States may face additional "downstream" losses from counterfeiting and piracy. IPR infringement could result in the loss of jobs that would have been created if the infringement did not occur, which could translate into lost earnings by U.S. workers and, in turn, lost tax revenues for federal, state, and local governments.[30] Attempts have been made in specific economic sectors to quantify the IPR infringement levels and related losses to legitimate U.S. businesses.

Overall U.S. Estimates

The BASCAP study (discussed in the international section) used its global findings to determine the impact of global counterfeiting and piracy on the United States (see **Table 3**). BASCAP estimated that the United States consumes $66-$100 billion in domestically produced counterfeit and pirated goods annually (based on 2008 data). In terms of specific industries, BASCAP estimated that the United States consumes $7-$20 billion worth of digitally pirated recorded music and $1.4-$2 billion in digitally pirated movies in 2005.

Table 3. Estimated U.S. Economic Losses due to Counterfeiting and Piracy (Billions of U.S. Dollars)

Category	Loss Estimate (based on 2008 data)
Internationally traded counterfeit and pirated products	$45-$60
Domestically produced and consumed counterfeit and pirated products	$12-$14
Digitally pirated products	$9-$25
Total	$66-$100

Source: Frontier Economics, *Estimating the Global Economic and Social Impacts of Counterfeiting and Piracy*, A Report Commissioned by Business Action to Stop Counterfeiting and Piracy (BASCAP), February 2011.

A private Commission on the Theft of American Intellectual Property estimates the total level of U.S. economic losses to international theft of U.S. intellectual property to be even higher, at hundreds of billions dollars per year. The Commission says the level of losses is comparable to the size of U.S. exports to Asia in 2012, valued at $320 billion.[31]

Sectoral Estimates

Attempts also have been made in some intellectual property-based industries to quantify the IPR infringement levels and related losses to legitimate U.S. businesses. For example, in prior years, IIPA, a U.S. copyright industry association, and PhRMA, a U.S. pharmaceutical industry association, have calculated estimates of losses to their member companies from IPR infringement. However, in recent years, neither of these industry groups has provided estimates. This may be, in part, because of the growing complexities in calculating the impact of such losses because of trends such as increased piracy taking place through the Internet.

THE ORGANIZATIONAL STRUCTURE OF IPR PROTECTION

Given the importance of intellectual property to the U.S. economy and the economic losses associated with counterfeiting and piracy, the United States is a leading advocate of strong global IPR rules. Since the mid-1980s, the United States has integrated IPR policy in its international trade policy activities, pursuing enhanced IPR laws and enforcement through multilateral, regional and bilateral trade agreements, and national trade laws.

Multilateral IPR System

World Trade Organization (WTO)

At the center of the present multilateral trading system is the World Trade Organization (WTO), an international organization established in 1995 as the successor to the General Agreements on Tariffs and Trade (GATT).[32] The WTO was established as the result of the Uruguay Round of trade negotiations (1986-1994), which led to agreements to liberalize and establish or enhance rules on trade in goods, services, agriculture, and other non-tariff barriers to trade. One of the Uruguay Round agreements was the Agreement on Trade-Related Aspects of Intellectual Property Rights (TRIPS Agreement), which sets minimum standards on intellectual property rights protection and enforcement with which all WTO member states must comply. The United States, the European countries, and the IPR business community were instrumental in including IPR on the Uruguay Round agenda. Many developing countries were wary of including IPR in trade negotiations, preferring to discuss them under the World Intellectual Property Organization (WIPO) (see below) instead. However, developing countries agreed, after being granted delayed compliance periods, and after achieving negotiating goals on other issues such as the end of quotas on textiles and clothing.

While previous international treaties on IPR continue to exist, the TRIPS Agreement was the first time that intellectual property rules were incorporated into the multilateral trading system. Two basic tenets of the TRIPS Agreement are national treatment (signatories must treat parties of other WTO members no less favorably in terms of IPR protection than the party's own nationals) and most-favored-nation treatment (any advantage in IPR protection granted to the party of another WTO member shall be granted to nationals of all other WTO member states).

Much of the TRIPS Agreement sets out the extent of the agreement's coverage of the various types of intellectual property: patents, copyrights, trademarks, trade secrets, geographical indications, industrial designs, layout of circuitry design, and test data. The TRIPS Agreement provisions build on several existing IPR treaties administered by the WIPO (discussed below). Another part provides standards of enforcement for IPR covered by the agreement. It enumerates standards for civil and administrative procedures and remedies, the application of border measures, and criminal procedures. A Council for the TRIPS Agreement was established to monitor the implementation of the agreement and transition arrangements were devised for developing countries. Finally, the agreement provides for the resolution of disputes under the Uruguay Round Agreement's Dispute Settlement Understanding (see **text box**). The binding nature of the WTO dispute settlement mechanism, with the possibility of the withdrawal of trade concessions (usually the reimposition of tariffs) for non-compliance, sets this agreement apart from previous IPR treaties that did not have effective dispute settlement mechanisms.

U.S. WTO Cases Against China on IPR

In April 2007, the United States filed two WTO dispute settlement cases against China, alleging inadequacies in China's enforcement of IPR laws and its barriers to market access for U.S. copyright businesses.[33]

In January 2009, the WTO issued its final ruling on the case centering on IPR enforcement issues. The WTO panel ruled in the United States' favor that China's denial of copyright protection to works without censorship approval is inconsistent with the TRIPS Agreement. The panel also agreed with the United States that it is impermissible for China to publicly auction IPR-infringing goods seized at the border, with the only requirement being that fake brands and trademarks be removed from the goods. The WTO panel ruled that more evidence was needed before deciding whether the thresholds for prosecution of counterfeiting and piracy in China's criminal law permit commercial scale IPR infringement. China agreed to implement the WTO ruling.[34]

In August 2009, a WTO panel ruled that a number of China's restrictions on trading rights and distribution of IPRrelated products were inconsistent with WTO rules. However, the WTO panel did not address whether China's censorship policies or import limitations on foreign films violate WTO rules. China agreed to implement the WTO ruling.[35]

The TRIPS Agreement also seeks a balance of rights and obligations between protecting private right holders and the obligation "to secure social and cultural development that benefits all."[36] Article 7 declares that

> ... the protection and enforcement of IPR should contribute to the promotion of technological innovation and to the transfer and dissemination of technology, to the mutual advantage of producers and users of technological knowledge and in a manner conducive to social and economic welfare and to a balance of rights and obligations.

This paragraph attempts to link the protection of IPR with greater technology transfer, including technology covered by IPR protection, to the developing world. The language itself has been interpreted in various ways. Developed countries have tended to consider this language exhortatory, but developing countries have tried, without much success, to make technology transfer a meaningful obligation within the TRIPS Agreement system. Article 66.2 of the agreement requires developed country members to provide incentives to their enterprises and institutions to promote technology transfer to least-developed countries to assist them in establishing a viable technology base. Developed countries report annually on their efforts to encourage technology transfer.

Complying with international IPR standards may impose greater burdens on developing countries than developed countries. Developing countries generally have to engage in greater efforts to bring their laws, judicial processes, and enforcement mechanisms into compliance with the TRIPS Agreement. Consequently, developing countries were given an extended period of time in which to bring their laws and enforcement mechanisms into compliance with the TRIPS Agreement. Developing countries and post-Soviet states were given an additional four years from the entry into force of the agreement (January 1, 1995). For products that were not covered by a country's patent system (such as pharmaceuticals in many cases), an additional five years was granted to bring such products under coverage. For developing countries, all provisions of the TRIPS agreement should now be in force. For the least developed countries, the phase-in period for IPR commitments was originally extended 10 years to January 1, 2006 (Article 66.1). In 2002, the WTO extended IPR obligations for least developed countries with respect to pharmaceuticals to January 1, 2016.[37] In addition, the WTO has extended the overall transitional period twice—in 2005, an extension to July 1, 2013, and then in 2013, a further extension to July 1, 2021.[38] Article 66.1 acknowledges the:

> special needs and requirements of least-developed country Members, their economic, financial and administrative constraints, and their need for flexibility to create a viable technological base.

Declaration on TRIPS Agreement and Public Health

In agreeing to launch the Doha Round of WTO trade negotiations, trade ministers adopted a "Declaration on the TRIPS Agreement and Public Health" on November 14, 2001.[39]

The Declaration sought to alleviate developing country dissatisfaction with aspects of the TRIPS regime (see **text box**). It delayed the implementation of patent system provisions for pharmaceutical products for least developed countries until 2016. The declaration committed member states to interpret and implement the agreement to support public health and to promote access to medicines for all. The Declaration recognized certain "flexibilities" in the TRIPS agreement to allow each member to grant compulsory licenses[40] for pharmaceuticals and to determine what constitutes a national emergency, expressly including public health emergencies such as HIV/AIDS, malaria, and tuberculosis or other epidemics.

Intellectual Property Protection and Development

The controversy over the relationship between IPR and development was engaged by the advent of the TRIPS Agreement, which for the first time placed IPR obligations on developing countries. Some hold that expansion of IPR is an obstacle to growth and development in less advanced countries, while others maintain that IPR are beneficial to both developed and developing countries.

Some IPR critics believe that a strong IPR regime may reduce developing countries' access to technology from advanced countries by imposing relatively higher fees for technology licenses and production rights than would occur in the absence of IPR, limiting their innovation and economic growth and development. For instance, Japan, Singapore, Taiwan, and South Korea enhanced their technological abilities and developed their economies through "reverse engineering" of foreign technologies.

Others claim that IPR promote technology transfer through increased trade, foreign investment, and licensing in the long-run by making a country more attractive to foreign partners. A 2002 OECD study concluded that stronger IPR laws, particularly enhanced patent standards, may be associated with increased foreign direct investment (FDI) and trade for developing countries over time, with variation by industries and level of development.[41] For instance, India experienced an increase in foreign investment and technology transfer once it expanded its patent protection. However, in recent years, India has taken measures considered by the U.S. government and business leaders to be a "backsliding" on IPR commitments, raising concerns about the country's IPR and innovation environment. China offers a counterexample of a country that, despite some improvements, continues to have a weak IPR regime but high FDI and trade levels.

There is also evidence that IPR's impact on developing countries may vary by the level of development. One study suggests that IPR protection may offer more benefits for the more industrialized developing countries, such as Brazil and India, compared to other developing countries. Such industrializing economies could experience economic growth of as much as 0.5% annually through increased trade, FDI, and licensing.[42] Another study finds that rapid economic growth is associated with weak intellectual property regimes, but that developing countries with higher levels of per capita income may benefit economically from stronger IPR regimes.[43]

There is also concern that strengthened patent protection may drive up prices for medicines or delay the entry of generic drugs into the market, reducing access to HIV/AIDS treatments and other drugs. IPR supporters argue that strong IPR is critical to creating incentives for pharmaceutical innovations and suggest that reduced prices are no guarantee that needed goods will make it into the hands of individuals in developing countries due to political corruption, poverty, lack of health care, and poor social infrastructure.

Paragraph 6 of the Doha Declaration directed the WTO members to formulate a solution to a corollary concern, the use of compulsory licensing by countries with insufficient or inadequate manufacturing capability. Compulsory licenses are issued by governments to authorize the use or production of a patented item by a domestic party other than a patent holder. They are authorized by Article 31 of TRIPS, which places certain limitations on their use, scope, and duration. A provision that predominantly restricted production authorized by compulsory license to the domestic market became the focal point of the negotiations because it, in effect, conveys the right of compulsory licensing only to countries with the capability to manufacture a given product. Countries without a domestic manufacturing capability were essentially precluded from using this flexibility of the TRIPS agreement.

On the eve of the Cancun Ministerial in August 2003, WTO members agreed on a Decision[44] to waive the domestic market provision of the TRIPS article on compulsory licensing (Article 31(f)) for exports of pharmaceutical products for "HIV/AIDS, malaria, tuberculosis and other epidemics" to least developed countries and countries with insufficient manufacturing capacity. This Decision was incorporated as an amendment to the TRIPS agreement at the Hong Kong Ministerial in December 2005.

The amendment must be ratified by two-thirds of the 153 WTO member states. The deadline for ratification has been extended a number of times, most recently, until December 31, 2015.[45] Until then, the 2003 waiver continues in force. To date, the United States and 76 other WTO members have ratified the amendment.[46] This means another 25 countries must ratify the amendment to reach the two-thirds threshold.

The system established by the WTO allows least developed countries and countries without sufficient manufacturing capacity to issue a compulsory license to a company in a country that can produce such a product. After a matching compulsory license is issued by the producer country, the drug can be manufactured and exported subject to various notification requirements, as well as quantity and safeguard restrictions. While several exporting countries have established laws and procedures for implementing this system, only Rwanda has availed itself of the system to import HIV/AIDS medicines from a generic manufacturer in Canada.[47]

World Intellectual Property Organization (WIPO)

In addition to the WTO, the other main multilateral venue for addressing IPR issues is the World Intellectual Property Organization (WIPO), a specialized agency affiliated with the United Nations with its own executive, legislative, and budgetary powers. Established in 1970, following the entry into force of the 1967 WIPO Convention, WIPO is charged with fostering the effective use and protection of intellectual property globally. WIPO's mandate focuses exclusively on intellectual property, in contrast to the WTO's broader international trade mandate. WIPO's antecedents are the 1883 Paris Convention for the Protection of Industry Property and the 1886 Berne Convention for the Protection of Literary and Artistic Work. Most of the substantive provisions of these two treaties are incorporated in the WTO's TRIPS Agreement. WIPO's primary function is to administer a group of IPR treaties which put forth minimum standards for member states (see **Appendix A**). All international IPR treaties, save TRIPS, are administered by WIPO.

In order to address digital technology issues not dealt with in the TRIPS Agreement, WIPO established the WIPO Copyright Treaty (WCT) and WIPO Performance and Phonograms Treaty (WPPT) in 1996, oftentimes collectively referred to as the "WIPO Internet Treaties."[48] Recent WIPO efforts have focused on patent law. In June 2000, WIPO signatories adopted the Patent Law Treaty (PLT), which called for harmonization of patent procedures. This agreement went into force on April 28, 2005. Discussions began in May 2001 for the Substantive Patent Law Treaty (SPLT), which targets issues specifically related to patent grants, but were put on hold in 2006. Government leaders participating in the Group of 8 (G-8) meeting in July 2008 called for "accelerated discussions" of the SPLT.[49] While discussions remain stalled, the main focus of the WIPO's work in this area has been on "building a technical and legal resource base from which to hold informed discussions in order to develop a work program" on various patent issues.[50]

WIPO's other functions include assisting member states through training programs, legislative information, intellectual property institutional development, automation and office modernization efforts, and public awareness activities. WIPO's enforcement activities are more limited than those of the WTO. Through its Advisory Committee on Enforcement (ACE), WIPO cooperates with member states to promote international coordination on enforcement activities.

Free Trade Agreements

In recent years, the United States increasingly has focused on free trade agreements (FTAs) as an instrument to promote stronger IPR regimes by foreign trading partners. In general, the United States has viewed the TRIPS Agreement and WIPO-administered treaties as a minimum standard and has pursued higher IPR protection and enforcement levels through regional and bilateral FTAs. To date, the United States has entered into 14 FTAs with 20 countries.

Trade Promotion Authority and Negotiating Objectives

Under Trade Promotion Authority (TPA), Congress delegates its constitutional authority to regulate foreign commerce to the President to negotiate and enter into certain free trade agreements (FTAs). TPA also includes provisions allowing implementing bills for trade agreements to be considered under expedited legislative procedures (no amendment, up-or-down vote), provided the President follows the guidelines, negotiating objectives, reporting, and consultation requirements mandated by Congress.[51] IPR issues have become important negotiating objectives in grants of TPA; the most recent extension of that authority expired on July 1, 2007.

IPR negotiating objectives for FTAs were first enacted in trade promotion authority (then known as fast-track authority) by the Omnibus Trade and Competitiveness Act of 1988 (P.L. 100-418). The act sought enactment and enforcement of adequate IPR protection from negotiating partners. It also sought to strengthen international rules, dispute settlement, and enforcement procedures through the GATT and other existing intellectual property conventions.

This negotiating mandate led to the establishment of the TRIPS Agreement during the Uruguay Round and the IPR provisions in the North American Free Trade Agreement (NAFTA). In the period since the 1988 Act, the IPR provisions of NAFTA and the TRIPS agreement became the template for other bilateral or regional FTAs. Thus, the focus of IPR negotiating objectives shifted from creating to strengthening the IPR trade regime.

2002 Trade Promotion Authority

FTA negotiations concluded under the George W. Bush Administration were conducted under the Trade Promotion Authority Act of 2002 (P.L. 107-210). The principal negotiating objectives with regards to IPR included

- Furthering adequate and effective protection of IPA through accelerated and full implementation of the TRIPS agreement and by ensuring FTAs negotiated by the United States "reflect a standard of protection similar to that found in U.S. law"[52];
- Protecting IPR related to new technologies and distribution methods, and facilitating legitimate digital trade;
- Eliminating discriminatory treatment in the use and enforcement of IPR;

- Ensuring adequate rights holder protection through digital rights management practices; and
- Providing strong enforcement of IPR.

These IPR negotiating objectives were highly significant to the future contours of U.S. FTA negotiations. The objective to negotiate trade agreements in terms of IPR that "reflect a standard of protection similar to that found in U.S. law" led to the negotiation of provisions that go beyond the level of protection provided in the TRIPS agreement. Often referred to as "TRIPS-plus" provisions, these obligations include expanding coverage to new sectors; establishing more extensive standards of protection; and reducing the flexibility options available in TRIPS, such as with respect to compulsory licensing. Some of the new measures also address technological innovations that have come about since the TRIPS Agreement.

The objective to apply existing IPR protections to digital media reflected the changing nature of global commerce. The language sought to extend provisions for IPR protection to new and emerging technologies and methods of transmission and dissemination. The language also called for standards of enforcement to keep pace with technological change and allow right holders legal and technological protections for their works over the Internet and other new media.

May 10, 2007, Bipartisan Trade Agreement

On May 10, 2007, the Bush Administration and Congress concluded a bipartisan agreement on trade policy that addressed some Members' concerns about the implications of enhanced IPR on developing countries' ability to meet public health needs (commonly referred to as the "May 10th Agreement").[53] In particular, congressional leadership sought to ensure that pending FTAs allowed trading partners enough flexibility to meet their IPR obligations and to be able to promote access to life-saving medicines, while otherwise meeting their international IPR protection and enforcement obligations. IPR language previously negotiated in the FTAs with the developing countries of Peru, Panama, and Colombia subsequently was modified to reflect the agreement. Because South Korea is an industrialized country, the United States did not significantly scale-down the patent protection obligations in the U.S.-Korea FTA.

Possible TPA Renewal

TPA in the form of the Bipartisan Congressional Trade Priorities Act of 2014 (BCTPA) (H.R. 3830/S. 1900) was introduced on January 9, 2014. The principal negotiating objectives in BCTPA with regards to intellectual property rights are similar to those of the TPA in 2002 (see above).

In addition, a new objective in the proposed BCTPA seeks to negotiate the prevention and elimination of government involvement in violations of IPR such as cybertheft or piracy. A related protection of trade secrets and proprietary information collected by governments in the furtherance of regulations are contained in the negotiating objective on regulatory coherence.

Finally, the proposed legislation reaffirms the Declaration on the TRIPS Agreement and Public Health and adds language to "foster innovation and access to medicine." It does not specifically refer to the patent protection provisions found in the May 10, 2007, Bipartisan Trade Agreement (discussed above) and the added language seemingly could be used to justify including or excluding those provisions in future FTAs.

IPR in Current Trade Negotiations

Trans-Pacific Partnership FTA

The Obama Administration is conducting negotiations with participants in the Trans-Pacific Partnership (TPP) Agreement—Australia, Brunei, Canada, Chile, Japan, Malaysia, Mexico, New Zealand, Peru, Singapore and Vietnam.[54] The objective is to build a comprehensive, high-standard reciprocal agreement to reduce and eliminate trade barriers and establish rules and disciplines to govern trade and investment in the region, and to expand and strengthen U.S. economic ties with other participating countries in the region. Through the TPP, the United Seeks to build on already established FTAs with Australia, Canada, Chile, Mexico, Peru, and Singapore.[20]

The United States is negotiating strong IPR provisions in the TPP consistent with the TPA mandate to "reflect a standard of protection similar to that found in U.S. law." On the controversial issue of additional patent protection for pharmaceuticals (e.g., patent term extension, patent linkage, data protection), the United States reportedly has offered a plan similar to the May 10th provision: to allow for optional implementation for developing countries in the TPP and mandatory provisions for developed ones, although certain details have yet to be worked out.[55]

IPR reportedly has been one of the more controversial chapters in the TPP negotiating text. Significant disagreement reportedly continues to exist between and among the parties negotiating the TPP such as in the areas of:

- **Copyrights:** Debate over the extension of copyright term lengths, protection of temporary copies, fair use provisions, Internet services provider liability, and anti-circumvention protection;
- **Patents:** Debate over the ability to patent plants and animal life, the ability to patent new uses for an existing product (e.g, "evergreen" patents), and data exclusivity for biologics, among other issues; and
- **Enforcement:** Debate over criminal penalties for trademark counterfeit and copyright piracy, as well as *ex officio* powers to seize suspected counterfeit goods in transit.[56]

Transatlantic Trade and Investment Partnership FTA

The Obama Administration also is conducting negotiations with the European Union (EU) on a comprehensive and high-standard free trade agreement, referred to as the proposed Transatlantic Trade and Investment Partnership (TTIP).[57] The United States and EU both maintain strong IPR standards and generally prioritize IPR protection and enforcement as a key trade negotiating objective. However, a final report by the U.S.-EU High Level Working Group on Jobs and Growth, which recommended the launch of the transatlantic FTA negotiations, suggested that it may be difficult to reconcile differences on the IPR obligations that each side typically includes in its FTAs.[58] For example, protection and enforcement of geographical indications could be controversial in the negotiations. The EU seeks strong GI protection because of their commercial value to EU producers (e.g., Parmesan cheese, Parma ham, Feta cheese, and Champagne). The United States tends to protect GIs through trademark law, and expresses concern that the EU approach to GIs raises national treatment issues and adversely affects trademarks and widely accepted generic products.[59]

Stakeholders on both sides could raise issues about how to balance IPR protection and enforcement with other public policy goals, such as access to medicines in poor or developing countries and the free flow of information. At the same time, the TTIP could lead to rules on trade secrets, an area of U.S. and EU concern in light of increased instances of trade secret theft internationally, including through cybercrime.[60]

Anti-Counterfeiting Trade Agreement

The Anti-Counterfeiting Trade Agreement (ACTA), which was negotiated outside of the WTO by the United States and nearly 40 other primarily developed countries, is intended to build on the TRIPS Agreement, such as by addressing new IPR issues in the digital environment. Concluded in 2010, the ACTA has not entered into force. The agreement's prospects are in question, following the European Parliament's rejection of it in 2012, amid widespread protests by advocates of Internet free speech. The ACTA needs instruments of ratification, acceptance, or approval from six signatories in order to enter into force. To date, Japan is the only party that has submitted a formal instrument of approval. IPR issues considered in the ACTA negotiations have reemerged in in the TPP and TTIP negotiations, making the ACTA of continued congressional interest.

Central IPR Standards in U.S. FTAs

What follows is a discussion of some of the central patent and copyright standards sought in FTAs that are currently in force or have been signed by the United States (see **Appendix B**).[61]

Patents

Patent protection is arguably one of the most contentious areas of U.S. FTA negotiations on IPR issues. While the United States and other developed countries advocate for strong patent protections in order to promote innovation, there is concern that such stringent protections may delay developing countries' access to, and increase prices of, generic drugs. Other issues also have emerged in patent debates, such as with respect to the patentability of innovations related to plants and animals (see **text box**). Many of the FTAs in force include TRIPS-plus patent provisions, the most prominent of which are patent term length extensions, linkages between regulatory authority and patent status, data protection, compulsory licensing and parallel importation. The FTAs with Peru, Panama, and Colombia respond to the concerns of some Members of Congress over provisions that could restrict access to medicines in these countries and contain less ambitious standards for pharmaceutical patents, compared to previously negotiated FTAs. Pharmaceutical industry advocates express concern that this modification in patent protection in these FTAs may set a precedent for future FTA negotiations.[62] How these issues will be addressed in the proposed TPP and TTIP continue to evolve. Some key patent issues are discussed below.

Patent Term Extensions

Many FTAs include provisions for mandatory patent term length extensions beyond the TRIPS Agreement obligation of patent protection terms of twenty years from the filing date. These FTAs allow for extensions in cases of "unreasonable" delays in the issuance of patents due to regulatory review or administrative process, which lessen the effective 20-year term of patent protection. Patent holders contend that such measures enhance the ability of rights-holders to recoup the costs of research and development of new products. However, there is concern that patent term extensions may delay the entry of generic drugs into a market. In a modification of TRIPS-plus obligations, FTAs with Peru, Colombia, and Panama state that patent term restorations for pharmaceutical products are optional.

Patent Linkages

Patent linkage is a common provision in the trade agreements obtained by the United States. In general, the term "patent linkage" refers to the attachment of regulatory approval for the marketing of a drug with the status of a patent. If a patent exists, the Food and Drug Administration and its counterparts in other countries may not grant marketing approval for a generic version of a drug that is patented in the country without the permission of the patent holder. The notion of patent linkage presents a departure from the minimum standards under TRIPS, under which generic drug manufacturers are able to apply for marketing approval without the patent owner's permission and prior to the expiration of the patent; this may reduce the time it takes for generic drugs to enter a market once the patent expires.[63] In light of developing country concerns about delays in access to generic versions of drugs, FTAs signed with Peru, Panama, and Colombia do not tie marketing approval for a generic drug with the patent status of its brand name drug.

Data Protection

In cases in which the patent holders must submit undisclosed data regarding the safety or efficacy of new pharmaceutical or agricultural products (such as data from clinical trials) in order to market them, the TRIPS Agreement requires members to take measures to protect such data from disclosure and unfair commercial use. The TRIPS Agreement does not prescribe any time period for this protection. Recent U.S. FTAs generally require a five-year period of marketing exclusivity for the patent holder, which typically begins from the date the product is approved in the country. Under this TRIPS-plus provision, generic drug manufacturers who want to market and distribute a generic version of a drug while the data exclusivity period is in effect must conduct their own clinical trials and submit their own findings to the national drug regulatory authority; they cannot rely on the findings submitted by the patent holder. On one hand, clinical trials and other testing used to develop the data submitted for marketing approval can be costly and take years to develop, and thus, adequate protection of test data is important as an incentive for future investments in such R&D. On the other hand, such provisions may raise the cost of manufacturing generic versions of patented drugs, as well as delay access to generic forms of drugs. The FTAs with Peru, Panama, and Colombia include provisions that may reduce data exclusivity terms of five years by a minimum of six months in practice.[64]

Compulsory Licensing

A compulsory license is an authorization by a government for third parties (such as a company or the government itself) for the manufacture or use of a product under patent without the permission of the rights- holder. The TRIPS Agreement permits signatories to issue compulsory licenses for patented devices and provide compensation to the owner of the patent and does not limit the situations in which such licenses may be issued. The third party must have attempted to obtain permission from the patent holder, although this requirement is waived in times of national emergency or other extenuating circumstances. U.S. FTAs with Australia and Singapore limit attaining compulsory licenses only for domestic use and to situations of remedying antitrust violations or in situations of public non-commercial use, national emergency, or other cases of extreme need. Also under these FTAs, the patent holder is under no obligation to provide test data, technical know-how or other undisclosed information for the patent subject to compulsory license. The compulsory license provisions have not been included in FTAs with developing countries. In addition, the U.S.-Korea FTA (KORUS) does not place any specific limitations on compulsory licensing.

Parallel Importation

Parallel imports, also known as grey-market goods, refer to goods imported into a country without permission of the rights-holder after those goods were legitimately sold elsewhere. Parallel importation relates to the concept of territorial exhaustion of IPR, which governs the extent of IPR after the first sale. Under a national system of exhaustion practiced in the United States, IPR are exhausted domestically after the first sale, but not abroad, thus prohibiting trade in those goods without permission of the rights-holder. Under an international system, IPR are exhausted at the first sale for any destination, and such goods can be exported freely. Article 6 of the TRIPS specifically excludes issues arising from exhaustion of IPR from WTO dispute settlement, allowing each member to adopt different exhaustion regimes. Thus, TRIPS does not address the issue of parallel imports. Some developing countries contend that parallel importation is an alternative method for governments to increase access to medicines in the absence of a compulsory license.[65] Pharmaceutical companies have voiced concerns that this practice threatens their ability to engage in price differentiation between different markets. U.S. FTAs negotiated with Australia, Singapore, and Morocco disallow parallel importing of patented products. Subsequent U.S. negotiated FTAs have not included this provision, due to language included in the Science, State, Justice, and Commerce, and Related Agencies, Appropriations Act of 2006 (P.L. 109-108), which prohibited the use of such provisions.

Biodiversity and Traditional Knowledge

International trade negotiations increasingly have focused on the protection of plant and animal inventions, new plant varieties, traditional knowledge, and folklore. Some indigenous communities in developing countries and international non-governmental organizations have expressed concern about the use of patents to provide private rights for traditional knowledge and genetic material; the commercial use of such resources by entities other than the indigenous communities or countries from which such resources are derived; and the distribution of benefits from commercial use. The United States, other advanced countries, and business groups favor treating traditional knowledge and genetic material as intellectual property and protecting these resources through an IPR framework.

Article 27.3(b) of the TRIPS Agreement permits Member states to exempt "plants and animals other than microorganisms, and essentially biological processes" from patentability. TRIPS requires Members to protect plant varieties through patent protection, some other system ("sui generis"), or a combination of the two. Paragraph 19 of the Doha Declaration added another dimension to the issue by requiring the TRIPS Council to probe the relationship between the TRIPS Agreement, the UN Convention on Biological Diversity (CBD), and traditional knowledge and folklore.

These issues also are being discussed in WIPO's Intergovernmental Committee on Intellectual Property and Genetic Resources, Traditional Knowledge, and Folklore (IGC).

India, Brazil, and Peru, among other countries, contend that patent applicants should be required to disclose the source of genetic materials, including plant life and traditional knowledge, before obtaining patents. The United States and the European Union have advocated for national systems in which companies are granted permission to research genetic materials and are obligated to share benefits from patents derived from those genetic products.

Some earlier U.S. FTAs have required signatories to provide protection for plants, animals, and plant varieties. The recent FTAs with Peru, Panama, and Colombia do not mandate patentability for plants and animals, but state that the countries should take efforts to expand patent coverage to these areas and to maintain this protection once it is offered. Side-letters in the three FTAs state the signatories' recognition of the importance of biodiversity and traditional knowledge and pledge the countries to work together to address these issues through the IGC.

Copyright

In the area of copyright protection, the United States has pursued certain TRIPS-plus measures in FTAs, such as extending copyright terms; including anti-circumvention provisions; and protecting rights-management information in its FTAs. The TRIPS Agreement does not mention any obligations regarding rights-management information, which is "electronic information that identifies a protected work, its author, and terms and conditions of use,"[66] perhaps due to the fact these technologies were not available at the time. In contrast, U.S.-negotiated trade agreements prohibit the removal or alteration of such information.

While patent protection has experienced policy shifts in the FTAs with Peru, Panama, and Colombia, copyright protection provisions have remained fairly consistent through the FTAs. In general, FTA signatories are obligated to provide an additional twenty years of copyright protection. This brings the minimum copyright term to seventy years from the death of the author or authorized publication, compared to fifty under the TRIPS Agreement. Responding to technological innovations not discussed in the TRIPS Agreement, many of the FTAs require trading partners to outlaw circumvention of technological measures protecting access to copyrighted works. These provisions build on the U.S. Digital Millennium Copyright Act

(DMCA) of 1998.[67] Also based on the DMCA, many FTAs contain provisions that regulate the liability of Internet service providers (ISPs) for copyright infringement that occurs within their networks. Under the FTAs, ISPs are provided limited immunity from copyright liability in certain kinds of infringing activities if they comply with regulations. For instance, ISPs must block access to or remove infringing materials as soon as they are aware of the infringement. Copyright holders argue that it is necessary for ISPs to assist in enforcing copyright for copyright laws to be effective. However, critics claim that these provisions impose excessive burdens on ISPs, reduce the rights of Internet users, and limit the policy flexibility of FTA signatories in determining their own IPR regimes.

Trade Secrets

A company's ability to protect its commercially valuable proprietary information may affect its competitiveness or even its survival. Such proprietary information can include blueprints, production processes, marketing strategies, or sales information. In its *2013 Special 301 Report* (discussed below), USTR described the protection of U.S. trade secrets as a growing challenge threatening the economic security of the United States. The report responded to concerns of U.S. business that governments have pressured them to reveal trade secrets or to transfer technology to further a country's 'indigenous innovation' policies. Companies are also reportedly increasingly victimized by outright theft of their trade secrets, and have decried the often lax remedies available to combat such theft. Trade secret theft has taken on new and increased complexities in the digital environment, and the United States is increasingly concerned about trade secret theft through cybercrime. Penalties for trade secret theft vary widely among countries; some countries have no penalties at all while others have civil remedies or criminalize trade secret theft that results from computer hacking. In the United States, remedies for trade secret theft primarily are found in state law.[68]

While the U.S. aim in the intellectual property chapters of the TPP seeks to establish criminal penalties for the theft of trade secrets, it may pursue aspects of this agenda through other trade negotiations or means of economic statecraft. Such an agenda may involve prohibiting countries from: (1) conditioning market access on technology transfer; (2) seeking concessional terms for acquiring or licensing IPR by state-owned enterprises (SOEs); (3) requiring the use of locally owned or developed IPR; (4) promoting the development of local standards to unfairly advantage local firms; and (5) requiring the unnecessary disclosure of confidential business information, or failing to protect such information. The Obama Administration's strategy on mitigating the theft of U.S. trade secrets, released in February 2013, underscores U.S. interest in seeking, in U.S. trade negotiations, new criminal remedy provisions for trade secret theft—similar to remedies provided in U.S. law.[69]

New and Evolving Issues

U.S. trade policy also increasingly is focused on addressing new and evolving issues in international IPR protection and enforcement. The IPR landscape is changing, both due to the growing role of emerging markets in the global marketplace and the increased level of international trade taking place in the digital environment. Some of these issues are discussed below.

Indigenous Innovation

Originally associated with China, "indigenous innovation" is a term that can reflect multiple policy goals, including promoting innovation from domestic companies rather than relying on foreign technology, building domestic R&D capabilities, and increasing the share of overall value added by domestic companies to the domestic economy. Such innovation policies can surface in areas such as government procurement, technical standards, and technology transfer.[70] For example, indigenous innovation policies may require the transfer of technology as a condition for allowing access to a market or for a company to continue to do business in the market.[71] While the goal of increasing domestic manufacturing and innovation is understandable, the U.S. government, industry groups, and other stakeholders express concern that indigenous innovation policies are discriminatory and may unfairly disadvantage U.S. right holders in those countries. China's indigenous innovation policies, for example, have been a source of trade tension with the United States. Although the Chinese government has pledged to separate indigenous innovation from government procurement, U.S. business leaders remain concerned that China's policies may lead to discrimination against foreign firms or run afoul of WTO commitments.[72] While China's indigenous innovation policies remain a focal point of U.S. trade policy, according to the USTR's *2013 Special 301 Report*, such policies appear to be gaining ground in other countries as well, such as India.

Localization Barriers to Trade

Functioning as a type of non-tariff barrier to market access, "forced" localization measures generally refer to those designed to protect, favor, or stimulate domestic industries, service providers, or intellectual property at the expense of foreign counterparts. Localization barriers can take a number of forms, such as requirements for: service providers to process data in the foreign country as a condition of market access; businesses to transfer technology and intellectual property as a condition of approval of foreign investments; or firms to use local content as a condition for manufacturing or for government procurement. For example, in November 2011, India issued a "National Manufacturing Policy," which calls for greater local content requirements in government procurement in certain sectors, such as information and communications technology and clean energy. India's National Manufacturing Policy is rooted in the country's goal of developing its manufacturing base and boosting employment. Based on this policy, in recent years, the Indian government has undertaken or is considering undertaking a series of regulatory measures mandating the use of local goods and services in business activity in India, across a range of industrial sectors. While some localization barriers may serve data privacy or security objectives, concerns have arisen that some of these measures can be economically distorting. According to the USTR, these measures can distort trade, inhibit FDI, and lead other countries to follow suit.[73] Certain localization barriers have been addressed in previous multilateral trade negotiations. For instance, the WTO Agreement on Trade-Related Investment Measures (TRIMs) prohibits "local content" requirements imposed in a discriminatory manner with respect to foreign investment.[74] Other localization barriers, particularly with respect to the digital environment, are considered to be newer trade issues, and are a focus of the TPP and TTIP negotiations.

Patent Revocation, Denial and Changes in Thresholds of Patentability

U.S. policymakers, business leaders, and other are increasingly concerned about policy and legal developments in various countries that, from their perspective, are leading to a deterioration of patent protections. Key issues have been raised about provisions in India's Patent Law that prohibit patents on certain chemical forms absent a showing of increased efficacy. According to the USTR, this practice could limit the patentability of potentially beneficial innovations (see **text box**).

Recent Pharmaceutical Patent Decisions in India

Since 2012, India has denied or revoked patents for several cancer and hepatitis C drugs developed by several Western pharmaceutical companies, including Bayer, GSK, Novartis, Pfizer, and Roche. India's Supreme Court has decided to prohibit patents for certain chemical forms absent a showing of "enhanced efficacy," although the products are protected by patents in many other countries. India's patent laws are designed to protect against "ever-greening," a practice by which an innovator pharmaceutical company seeks a patent on a modified version of the originally patented drug to extend the life of the patent, unless there is a showing of enhanced efficacy. Some argue that through ever-greening, pharmaceutical companies make minor modifications to their patents solely to extend their monopoly on the patent, thus, delaying the entry of lower-cost generic versions of the drugs onto the market. Others argue that the modifications can provide new benefits, such as "fewer side effects, decreased toxicity, and better delivery systems."[75] India also has issued, or threatened to issue, compulsory licenses for pharmaceuticals. For example, in March 2012, the Indian government issued a compulsory license to an Indian pharmaceutical company to produce a generic version of Nexavar, a kidney cancer drug produced by Bayer. India defended its decision on the basis that the price for the patented drug was too high for most Indians. In other developments, the Indian government "hinted" it would revoke the patent on Herceptin, a breast cancer drug developed by Roche. In August 2013, Roche withdrew the patent for the drug in India.[76]

Another country of concern is Canada. The USTR noted concerns about Canadian courts' recent decisions regarding the heightened "utility" requirement for pharmaceutical patents. U.S. pharmaceutical companies argue that such decisions contribute to an uncertain business environment in Canada. For example, one U.S. pharmaceutical company challenged Canada under NAFTA's Chapter 11 investor-state dispute settlement mechanism, based on a Canadian court's decision to invalidate the company's patent (see **text box**).

The Eli Lilly-Canada Chapter 11 Case

USTR has criticized the interpretation of utility in judicial invalidation of pharmaceutical patents, which has led to a NAFTA Chapter 11 investor-state dispute settlement case.[77]

The U.S. pharmaceutical company Eli Lilly has filed a Notice of Arbitration against the Government of Canada seeking damages in the amount of $500 million in lost sales stemming from the invalidation of patents for two medicines. In Canada, the patents for 18 drugs have been invalidated since 2002 through the use of the so-called promise doctrine, with an estimated loss of revenue to brand-name pharmaceutical companies of $1.1 billion.[78] This common law doctrine, first invoked by the Supreme Court of Canada in 2002, states that the utility of a patent must be demonstrated or soundly predicted in the patent application. Lilly claims that this standard is discriminatory, contrary to utility standards in other countries and in NAFTA itself, and is adverse to Canada's own interpretation of utility at the time of NAFTA signing.[79] This standard, some argue, makes it easier for generic companies to challenge the usefulness of a patented drug. The Government of Canada is currently assessing the information provided in the Notice of Arbitration filed by Eli Lilly on September 12, 2013, and vows to vigorously defend itself against the claims. However, some observers have maintained that there is no uniform standard for utility among countries, and no one standard enshrined in NAFTA.[80]

U.S. TRADE LAW

Special 301

- Section 301 of the Trade Act of 1974 (P.L. 93-618), as amended, is the principal U.S. statute for identifying foreign trade barriers due to inadequate intellectual property protection. The 1988 Omnibus Trade and Competitiveness Act (P.L. 100-418) strengthened section 301 by creating "Special 301" provisions, which require the USTR to conduct an annual review of foreign countries' intellectual property policies and practices. By April 30th of each year, the USTR must identify countries that do not offer "adequate and effective" protection of IPR or "fair and equitable market access to United States person that rely upon intellectual property rights." According to an amendment to the Special 301 provisions by the Uruguay Round Agreements Act (P.L. 103-465), the USTR can identify a country as denying sufficient intellectual property protection even if the country is complying with its TRIPS commitments. These findings are submitted in the USTR's annual "Special 301" report.

- The USTR can designate countries in one of several statutorily- or administratively-created categories:
- **Priority Foreign Country:** A statutory category for those designated by the USTR as having "the most onerous or egregious acts, policies or practices that deny intellectual property protection and limit market access to U.S. persons or firms depending on intellectual property rights protection" and the "greatest adverse impact (actual or potential) on the relevant United States products."

  These countries may be investigated under section 301 provisions of the Trade Act of 1974. The USTR cannot identify countries as Priority Foreign Countries if they have entered into good faith negotiations or have made significant progress in improving their intellectual property protection record.[81] If a country is named as a "Priority Foreign Country," the USTR must launch an investigation into that country's IPR practices. The USTR may suspend trade concessions and impose import restrictions or duties, or enter into a binding agreement with the priority country that would eliminate the act, policy, or practice that is the subject of the action to be taken. Since the WTO and its recourse to dispute settlement, the use of the first option may lead to the initiation of dispute settlement proceedings at the WTO for member countries, rather than unilateral retaliation. For the limited number of countries outside the WTO, trade sanctions remain a possibility.
- **Priority Watch List:** An administrative category created by the USTR for those countries whose acts, policies, and practices warrant concern, but who do not meet all of the criteria for identification as Priority Foreign Country. The USTR may place a country on the Priority Watch List when the country lacks proper intellectual property protection and has a market of significant U.S. interest.
- **Watch List:** An administrative category created by USTR to designate countries that have intellectual property protection inadequacies that are less severe than those on the Priority Watch List, but still attract U.S. attention.
- **Section 306 Monitoring.** A tool used by USTR to monitor countries for compliance with bilateral intellectual property agreements used to resolve investigations under section 301.

- **Out-of-Cycle Review.** A tool used by USTR on countries to monitor their progress on intellectual property issues, and which may result in status changes for the following year's Special 301 report.

For the *2013 Special 301 Report*, the USTR reviewed the IPR policies and practices of 95 countries, and designated them in one of the categories discussed above (see **Table 4**).

Table 4. USTR *2013 Special 301 Report*: Country Designations

Special 301 Category	2013 Special 301 Designation
Priority Foreign Country	• Ukraine—based on concerns of the country's continued deterioration in IPR protection, enforcement, and market access for persons relying on IPR; the first time in seven years that the USTR has listed a country. In May 2013, USTR announced that the United States has initiated an investigation under section 301 of the Trade Act of 1974 of the IPR acts, policies, and practices of Ukraine. However, in March 2014, the USTR announced that it would not take any action against Ukraine in light of its political situation.
Priority Watch List	10 countries: Algeria, Argentina, Chile, China, India, Indonesia, Pakistan, Russia, Thailand, and Venezuela
Watch List	30 countries: Barbados, Belarus, Bolivia, Brazil, Bulgaria, Canada, Colombia, Costa Rica, Dominican Republic, Ecuador, Egypt, Finland, Greece, Guatemala, Israel, Italy, Jamaica, Kuwait, Lebanon, Mexico, Paraguay, Peru, Philippines, Romania, Tajikistan, Trinidad and Tobago, Turkey, Turkmenistan, Uzbekistan, and Vietnam
Section 306 Monitoring	China and Paraguay
Out-of-Cycle Reviews	• Spain—focusing on steps to combat copyright piracy over the Internet • El Salvador—focusing on implementation of new legislation on pharmaceuticals and enforcement efforts • "notorious markets"—including online markets, that reportedly engage in piracy and counterfeiting

Source: CRS adaption from USTR, *2013 Special 301 Report*; and USTR, "Notice of Determination in Section 301 Investigation of Ukraine," 79 *Federal Register* 14326, March 13, 2014.

Notes: For the *2013 Special 301 Report*, the USTR reviewed the IPR policies and practices of 95 countries, and designated them in one of several categories.

The Special 301 statute provides the overall guideline for identifying countries for the various lists. However, placement on one of the lists is country-specific and takes into consideration a host of factors, including the level and scope of the country's IPR infringement and their impact on the U.S. economy, the strength of the country's IPR laws and enforcement of IPR laws, progress made by the country in improving IPR protection and enforcement in the past year, and the sincerity of the country's commitment to multilateral and bilateral trade agreements. There is no "weighting criteria" for the factors or a formula to determine the placement of a country on the watch list. Furthermore, no particular threshold exists for determining when a country should be upgraded or downgraded on the list. In making determinations, the USTR gathers information based on its annual trade barriers reports, as well as consultations with a wide variety of sources, including industry groups, other private sector representative, Congress, and foreign governments.

Section 337

Section 337 of the Tariff Act of 1930 (19 U.S.C. 1337), as amended, prohibits unfair methods of competition or other unfair acts in the importation of products into the United States. It also prohibits the importation of articles that infringe valid U.S. patents, copyrights, processes, trademarks, semiconductor products produced by infringing a protected mask work (e.g., integrated circuit designs), or protected design rights. While the statute has been utilized to counter imports of products judged to be produced by unfair competition, monopolistic, or anticompetitive practices, it has become increasingly used for its IPR enforcement functions in recent years. Under the statute, the import or sale of an infringing product is illegal only if a U.S. industry is producing an article covered by the relevant IPR or is in the process of being established. However, unlike other trade remedies such as antidumping or countervailing duty actions, no showing of injury due to the import is required.

The U.S. International Trade Commission (ITC) administers section 337 proceedings. USITC must investigate complaints either brought to it or ones commenced under its own initiative. An administrative law judge provides an initial determination to the ITC which can accept the initial determination or order a further review of it in whole or in part. If the ITC finds a violation, it may issue two types of remedies: exclusion orders or cease and desist orders. The ITC may issue either a limited or general exclusion order enforced by

U.S. Customs and Border Protection (CBP). A general exclusion order directs CBP to keep out all infringing articles regardless of the source. More commonly, a limited exclusion order is employed to exclude infringing articles from the firm subject to the ITC's investigation. Alternatively, the ITC may enforce a cease and desist order to stop the sale of the infringing product in the United States. However, the ITC may consider several public interest criteria and decline to issue a remedy. Also, the President may disapprove a remedial order during a 60 day review period for "policy reasons." A presidential review of a remedial order often considers several relevant factors, including "(1) public health and welfare; (2) competitive conditions in the U.S. economy; (3) production of competitive articles in the United States; (4) U.S. consumers; and (5) U.S. foreign relations, economic and political."[82]

The number of Section 337 cases managed by the ITC has trended upward in recent years. The overwhelming majority of Section 337 cases are patent-focused, involving high-technology products, such as telecommunication and computer equipment (e.g., smartphones and tablets); integrated circuits (e.g., memory chips); and display devices (e.g., digital televisions). Other investigations concerned consumer items, and chemical and medical technologies. In addition, in FY2012, the ITC saw an increase in the number of investigations involving alleged misappropriation of trade secrets related to imported goods.[83]

In the 112th Congress, legislative efforts related to Section 337 focused on addressing jurisdictional problems associated with holding foreign websites accountable for piracy and counterfeiting. Multiple bills were introduced, renewing congressional and public debate about the balance between protecting U.S. intellectual property and promoting innovation. Congress could take these issues up again, as well as other issues, including CBP's enforcement of Section 337 exclusion orders.

Generalized System of Preferences

The Generalized System of Preferences (GSP) is a program that provides preferential duty-free entry to certain products from designated developing countries. The purpose of the program is to foster economic growth in developing countries by increasing their export markets. The Trade Act of 1974 authorized the GSP for a ten-year time frame, and the program has been renewed from time to time. The GSP program expired in 2013, and legislation considering its renewal could be considered by Congress.[84]

Although the GSP is non-reciprocal, it can be used to promote stronger intellectual property protection and enforcement abroad. Under the GSP statute, the President must consider a set of mandatory criteria that a country must fulfill in order to be designated as a GSP beneficiary. Additionally, the President may evaluate a country on the basis of certain discretionary criteria, including the country's provision of IPR protection.[85]

The GSP program undergoes an annual review by the GSP Subcommittee of the Trade Policy Staff Committee (TPSC), which is headed by the USTR. As part of its evaluation, the TPSC addresses concerns about specific country practices (such as intellectual property protection) and makes recommendations to the President. Following the 2012 GSP Annual Review, the USTR has decided to continue to review IPR practices in Indonesia, Russia, Ukraine, and Uzbekistan, on the basis of IIPA petitions for ongoing GSP reviews.[86]

ISSUES FOR CONGRESS

Congress has legislative, oversight, and appropriations responsibilities related to IPR and trade policy. What follows are certain key issues that Congress could consider as it fulfills those responsibilities.

U.S. Efforts to Promote IPR through Trade Policy

Since the inclusion of IPR provisions in NAFTA and the TRIPS Agreement, IPR protection and enforcement have been major U.S. trade policy negotiating objectives. Alongside the growing role of IPR in trade policy, there has been an ongoing debate regarding the appropriateness of this role. From one perspective, IPR could promote trade through innovation, economic growth, and technology transfer from advanced to developing countries. From another perspective, IPR, which grant legal temporary monopolies to rights holders for their creations, could be considered barriers to trade with no place in trade liberalization negotiations. Given the continued use of trade policy to advance IPR objectives, debates also have focused on the appropriate balance between the protection and enforcement of IPR and other public policy objectives, such as access to medicines and the free flow of information, as well as the extent to which these goals are complementary or conflicting. Additionally, there have been debates about the trade policy channels used by the United States to promote IPR goals. Some question the appropriateness of using regional and bilateral FTAs for pursuing stronger IPR, contending that such actions take away from the effectiveness of multilateral IPR promotion efforts. Others argue that strong IPR commitments in U.S. regional and bilateral FTAs can provide momentum for developing such disciplines at the multilateral level.

U.S. IPR negotiating objectives may be affected by the language of any future TPA. In discussions about renewal of TPA, Congress may choose to consider possible reiteration or expansion on its IPR goals related to global health from the 2002 TPA. Congress also may choose to consider whether or not to follow the template provided by the Peru, Panama, and Colombia FTAs in future trade negotiations, such as negotiations on the Trans-Pacific Partnership Agreement. In addition, through the debate over TPA negotiating objectives, Congress is expressing concerns over new and emerging issues in IPR, such as those related to indigenous innovation, "forced" localization barriers to trade in the digital environment, and cybercrime.

Addressing IPR Trade Challenges in Emerging Economies

Some policymakers have voiced concern over the effectiveness of the current U.S. trade policy agenda in addressing IPR trade challenges associated with emerging economies, such as China, India, and Brazil—countries with which there are no existing U.S. FTAs and with which the United States is currently not negotiating any FTAs. Congress could examine how existing trade policy tools are operating with respect to emerging economies. Beyond this, Congress could explore other options for advancing U.S. IPR trade policy objectives in emerging economies, including in the following areas:

- **U.S. FTA negotiations.** The TPP and TTIP negotiations are intended to help shape global rules addressing challenges in third countries, such as with respect to localization barriers to trade—issues relevant to emerging economies. Moreover, TPP negotiators seek to craft the TPP as an "open" and "living" agreement that other countries, such as China and India, could ultimately join if they were willing to take on its high standard commitments. Congress could consider to what extent the United States can or should encourage these emerging economies to join the TPP negotiations, and if so, how that might be accomplished.

- **Bilateral Investment Treaties (BITs).** Through the negotiation of BITs, the United States seeks to reduce barriers to foreign investment and strengthen protections for foreign investment.[87] The U.S. Model BIT, the template the United States uses to negotiate BITs and investment chapters of FTAs, treats IPR as a covered form of investment subject to protections. Currently, the United States is negotiating BITs with both China and India. Congress could examine the progress of these negotiations, including how IPR issues are being addressed. Should these BIT negotiations be concluded, they would be subject to Senate ratification in order to enter into force.
- **U.S. trade promotion and preference programs.** Some stakeholders point to U.S. trade promotion and preference programs as a potential tool for Congress to encourage policy reform in emerging economies. For example, in light of heightened concern over India's intellectual property environment, some stakeholders have called on Congress to remove India from the Generalized System of Preferences beneficiary list.[88] Should Congress take up GSP reauthorization, India's eligibility status could be among the issues examined.
- **WTO TRIPS Agreement.** Congress may examine how the WTO TRIPS Agreement is working with respect to emerging economies, as well as whether there are additional opportunities for seeking redress for violations of TRIPS Agreement commitments through the WTO Dispute Settlement Mechanism with these trading partners. For instance, the United States has seen some success in challenging China's copyright practices through the WTO. Some stakeholders also call for the United States to pursue greater trade enforcement action on IPR with respect to other countries.

Effectiveness of the U.S. IPR Organizational Structure

The United States has a complex apparatus for supporting intellectual property rights, with responsibilities cutting across many different federal government agencies. For an overview of federal agencies and coordinating bodies involved in U.S. IPR-related efforts, see **Appendix C**. Some Members of Congress, private sector representatives, and other stakeholders express concern about whether the present U.S. IPR organizational structure is doing enough to enforce foreign countries' IPR obligations, as well as whether the structure is capable of doing more.

One set of issues centers on coordination. Given the range of federal agencies involved in IPR protection and enforcement, questions have emerged about whether federal IPR activities are sufficiently coordinated in the present U.S. IPR organizational structure (see text box). On one hand, the Administration's establishment of various interagency bodies related to IPR, such as the Intellectual Property Enforcement Coordinator (IPEC), National Intellectual Property Rights Coordination Center (NIPRCC), and Interagency Trade Enforcement Center (ITEC), affirms the U.S. commitment to enforcing IPR and the importance of interagency coordination. On the other hand, there are debates about whether the various IPR-related interagency coordinating mechanisms overlap. From one perspective, these interagency bodies focus on differing aspects of IPR protection and enforcement, and in doing so, collectively help to advance U.S. IPR goals in trade policy. From another perspective, the existence of multiple interagency coordinating bodies can contribute to additional bureaucracy.

2013 Joint Strategic Plan on Intellectual Property Enforcement

The U.S. Intellectual Property Enforcement Coordinator (IPEC), assisted by its Advisory Committee, is charged with developing a "Joint Strategic Plan" for combating counterfeiting and piracy. Legislation requires the Joint Strategic Plan to include in its objectives: reducing counterfeiting and infringing goods in the domestic and international supply chain, identifying and addressing barriers to effective enforcement domestically, ensuring that information is shared among the relevant departments and agencies, eliminating domestic and international counterfeiting and infringement networks, strengthening the capacity of foreign countries to protect and enforce IPR, and cooperating with other countries to establish international standards and policies to enforce IPR. In June 2013, the IPEC released its second Joint Strategic Plan on Intellectual Property Enforcement, which noted progress and areas for future activity in six major areas of focus: (1) leading by example; (2) increasing transparency; (3) ensuring efficiency and coordination; (4) enforcing U.S. rights internationally; (5) securing the supply chain; and (6) building a data-driven government.

Source: Executive Office of the President, *2013 Joint Strategic Plan on Intellectual Property Enforcement*, June 2013 http://www.whitehouse.gov /sites/default/files/omb/IPEC/2013-us-ipec-joint-strategic-plan.pdf.

Another set of issues centers on federal resources for IPR protection and enforcement. While protection and enforcement of IPR is a stated trade policy priority for the United States, it is difficult to get a sense of the magnitude of federal funding and resources devoted to it. Some U.S. government agencies do not have a separate budgetary line item for IPR-related activities, and Congress does not always designate specific funds for IPR activities in its appropriations for agencies. Additionally, there is limited information on the economic and other impacts of piracy and counterfeiting on the United States. This may complicate the ability of lawmakers to weigh the threat of IPR infringement against the federal resources available for IPR and other government priorities. Furthermore, there could be debates about whether attempts to enhance interagency coordination, without devoting greater resources to IPR enforcement activities, may translate into greater U.S. IPR enforcement.

LOOKING FORWARD

U.S. efforts to protect and enforce IPR through U.S. trade policy are likely to continue to be of interest for Congress. The reliance on IPR as a competitive advantage to drive an innovative U.S. economy is reflected in U.S. trade policy. Congress may set the course of U.S. trade policy concerning IPR through the development of negotiating objectives in any future trade promotion authority. It also may consider the treatment of IPR in ongoing U.S. negotiations of the Trans-Pacific and Trans-Atlantic FTAs. It may weigh the balance between greater intellectual property rights in free trade agreements and the ability to conclude agreements containing such provisions with other countries. It may wish to examine how to incorporate the IPR aspects of new issues such as digital trade in U.S. policy.

Congress may also wish to examine the enforcement of U.S. IPR through existing trade agreements. Congress may examine the effectiveness of such activities such as Special 301. Congressional debates may continue in areas such as how IPR protection and enforcement relate to other public policy goals, such as access to affordable medicines. Congress may also wish to examine the organizational structure for IPR protection and the priority to place on such enforcement when allocating budgetary resources.

APPENDIX A. SUMMARY OF WIPO TREATIES

Treaty	Date Concluded	Provisions
Intellectual Property Protection Treaties		
Paris Convention for the Protection of Industrial Property (Paris Convention)	1883 (entered into force 1884)	Protects industrial property (includes patents, marks, industrial designs, utility models, trade names, and geographic indications)
Berne Convention for the Protection of Literary and Artistic Works (Berne Convention)	1886 (entered into force 1886)	Protects literary and artistic works, providing right to control and receive payments for use
Madrid Agreement for the Repression of False and Deceptive Indications of Source on Goods (Madrid Agreement - Indications of Source)	1891	Requires States to seize imported goods with false/deceptive indications of source or to prohibit importation of such goods; open to States party to Paris Convention (1883)
Rome Convention for the Protection of Performers, Producers of Phonograms and Broadcasting Organizations (Rome Convention)	1961	Protects rights of performers against certain acts to which they have not agreed; protects rights of producers of phonograms, and broadcasting organizations to authorize/prohibit certain acts; open to States party to Berne Convention (1886)
Convention for the Protection of Producers of Phonograms Against Unauthorized Duplication of their Phonograms (Phonograms Convention)	1971	Protects producers of phonograms against unauthorized reproduction of their phonograms or importation of duplications for public distribution
Brussels Convention Relating to the Distribution of Programme-Carrying Signals Transmitted by Satellite (Brussels Convention)	1974	Protects against the unauthorized distribution of program-carrying signals transmitted by satellite
Nairobi Treaty on the Protection of the Olympic Symbol (Nairobi Treaty)	1981	Protects Olympic symbol against unauthorized commercial uses

Appendix A. (Continued)

Treaty	Date Concluded	Provisions
Treaty on the International Registration of Audiovisual Works (Film Register Treaty)	1989	Establishes International Register for Audiovisual Works
Treaty on Intellectual Property in Respect to Integrated Circuits (Washington Treaty)	1989	Protects layout designs which display electrical components of an integrated circuit
Trademark Law Treaty (TLT)	1994	Streamlines national and regional trademark registration processes
WIPO Copyright Treaty (WCT)	1996 (entered into force 2002)	Special agreement under Berne Convention; grants exclusive rights to owners of copyright in computer programs and compilations of data/other material
WIPO Performances and Phonograms Treaty (WPPT)	1996 (entered nto force 2002)	Grants exclusive rights to performers and phonogram producers
Patent Law Treaty (PLT)	2000 (entered into 2005)	Aims to harmonize and streamline national and regional patent application procedures and patents
Singapore Treaty on the Law of the Trademarks	2006 (not yet in force)	Builds on TLT (1994); aims to harmonize trademark registration procedures; has wider scope (includes communication technology developments)
Beijing Treaty on Audiovisual Performances (Beijing Treaty)	2012 (not yet in force)	Seeks to strengthen economic rights of film actors and other performers through international standards.
Marrakesh Treaty to Facilitate Access to Published Works for Persons who are Blind, Visually Impaired or Otherwise Print Disabled (Marrakesh Treaty)	2013	Treaty to improve access to copyrighted works for the visually impaired and people with print disabilities

Treaty	Date Concluded	Provisions
Global Protection System Treaties		
Budapest Treaty on the International Recognition of the Deposit of Microorganisms for the Purposes of Patent Procedure (Budapest Treaty)	1977 (entered into force 1980)	Special agreement under Paris Convention (1883); requires States to recognize the deposit of a microorganism with any "international depositary authority"
Madrid Agreement Concerning the International Registration of Marks (Madrid Agreement - Marks)	1891	Requires seizure of imported goods with false/deceptive indication of source or prohibition of importation of such goods; open to States party to Paris Convention (1883)
Hague Agreement Concerning the International Registration of Industrial Designs (Hague Agreement)	1925 (entered into force 1928)	Allows protection of industrial designs in all member states on basis of single application with WIPO; three acts currently in force: 1934, 1960, and 1999 Acts
Lisbon Agreement for the Protection of Appellations of Origin and their International Registration (Lisbon Agreement)	1958	Provides international protection for geographical indications
Patent Cooperation Treaty (PCT)	1970 (entered into force 1978)	Establishes an international patent filing system; allows a single international patent application to have legal standing in all countries signatory to PCT; open to States party to Paris Convention (1883)
Protocol Relating to the Madrid Agreement (Madrid Protocol)	1989 (entered into force 1995)	Relates to Madrid Agreement (1891); seeks to make Madrid system more amenable to domestic laws of certain who are not yet signatories to Madrid Agreement; open to States party to Paris Convention (1883)

Appendix A. (Continued)

Treaty	Date Concluded	Provisions
Classification Treaties		
Nice Agreement Concerning the International Classification of Goods and Services of the Purposes of the Registration of Marks (Nice Agreement)	1957 (entered into force 1961)	Establishes a classification of goods and services in order to register trademarks and service marks; open to States party to Paris Convention (1883)
Locarno Agreement Establishing an International Classification for Industrial Designs	1968 (entered into force 1971)	Establishes a classification for industrial designs; open to States party to Paris Convention (1883)
Strasbourg Agreement Concerning the Industrial Patent Classification (Strasbourg Agreement)	1971 (entered into force 1975)	Establishes the International Patent Classification (IPC); open to States party to Paris Convention (1883)
Vienna Agreement Establishing Classification of the Figurative Elements of Marks (Vienna Agreement)	1973 (entered into force 1985)	Establishes a classification for marks which consist/contain figurative components; open to States party to Paris Convention (1883)

Source: WIPO.

APPENDIX B. PATENT AND COPYRIGHT PROVISIONS IN THE TRIPS AGREEMENT AND U.S. FTAS

Intellectual Property Forms	TRIPS Provisions (1994)	General TRIPS-Plus Provisions in FTAs	Scale-down of TRIPS-Plus Standards
Patents			
Patent term extensions	No provisions	Mandatory extensions in cases of unreasonable delays in patent grants/regulatory approval Jordan (Article 4.23.a), Chile (Article 17.9.6; 17.9.2a),	Optional extensions in cases of unreasonable delays in patent grants/regulatory approval NAFTA (Article 1709.12) Peru (Article 16.9.6),

Appendix B. (Continued)

Intellectual Property Forms	TRIPS Provisions (1994)	General TRIPS-Plus Provisions in FTAs	Scale-down of TRIPS-Plus Standards
		Singapore (Article 16.7.7; 18.8.4a), Australia (Article 17.9.8; 17.10.4), Morocco (Article 15.9.7; 15.10.3), CAFTA-DR (Article 15.9.6; 15.10.2), Bahrain (Article 14.8.6),Oman (Article 15.8.6), Korea (Article 18.8.6)	Panama (Article 16.9.6), Colombia (Article 16.9.6)
Market approval linked to patent status	No provisions NAFTA (no mention), Jordan (no linkage, but patent owner must be notified if another entity is seeking marketing approval for generic version of patented product, Article 4.23.b)	National regulatory authorities cannot provide marketing approval for a generic version of a patented drug without permission from rights-holder; also requires notification of rights-holder if marketing permitted Chile (Article 17.10.2b), Singapore (16.8.4c),Australia (Article 17.10.4), Morocco (Article 15.10.4), CAFTA-DR (Article 15.10.2), Bahrain (Article 14.9.4), Oman (15.9.4), Korea (Article 18.9.5)	Eliminates mandate that regulatory authorities cannot approve a generic drug for marketing if patent for drug in place Peru (Article 16.10.4), Panama (Article 15.10.4), Colombia (Article 16.10.4)

Intellectual Property Forms	TRIPS Provisions (1994)	General TRIPS-Plus Provisions in FTAs	Scale-down of TRIPS-Plus Standards
Protection for undisclosed test or other data	Members must protect data from unfair commercial use (Article 39.3) Jordan (Article 4.22)	Provides for at least five years of data exclusivity from date of approval in country for pharmaceuticals that contain new chemical products NAFTA (Article 1711.6), Bahrain (Article 14.9.1), Oman (Article 15.9(1-2), CAFTA-DR (Article 15.10.1), Singapore (Article 16.8(1-3)), Australia (Article 17.10.1), Morocco (Article 15.10.1), Chile (Article 17.10.1), Korea (Article 18.9(1-2))	Provides for at least five years of marketing exclusivity from date of approval in country of first filing if new drug is granted marketing approval within six months in country of second filing Peru (Article 16.10.2), Panama (Article 15.10.4), Colombia (Article 16.10.2)
Issuance of compulsory licenses	Some restrictions in issuance of compulsory licenses; circumstances under which licenses can be issued not limited (Article 13) *NAFTA (Article 1709.10),*	Limits issuance of compulsory license to specific cases: Correcting anti-competitive practices, public non-commercial contexts, national emergencies, and other extremely urgent situations *Jordan (Article 4.20), Singapore (Article 16.7.6), Australia (Article 17.9.7)*	Not discussed Chile (no mention), Morocco (no mention), CAFTA-DR (no mention), Bahrain (no mention), Oman (no mention) *Peru (no mention), Panama (no mention), Colombia (no mention), (no mention)*

Appendix B. (Continued)

Intellectual Property Forms	TRIPS Provisions (1994)	General TRIPS-Plus Provisions in FTAs	Scale-down of TRIPS-Plus Standards
Parallel importing of patented products	TRIPS will not be used to discuss IPR exhaustion (Article 6) Jordan (no mention), Chile (no mention), CAFTA-DR (no mention), Bahrain (no mention), Oman (no mention)	Parallel importation can be restricted or prohibited NAFTA (Article 1709.5, 1709.9), Singapore (Article 16.7.2), Morocco (Article 15.9.4), Australia (Article 17.9.4)	Not discussed Peru (no mention), Panama (no mention), Colombia (no mention), Korea (no mention)
Biodiversity and traditional knowledge	Members may exclude plants and animals from patentability (micro-organisms and non-biological and micro-biological processes must be eligible for patents); must provide protection of plant varieties (Article 27.3(b)) NAFTA (Article 1709.3), Bahrain (Article 14.8.(1-2)), Oman (Article 15.8.2, plants not discussed), Jordan, (no mention), Singapore	Countries shall make patents available for plants and animals Morocco (Article 15.9.2, plants and animals mentioned, plant varieties are not mentioned)	Members may exclude plants and animals from patentability, but shall take reasonable effort to provide patent protection for plants or animals and maintain protection once offered Chile (Article 17.9.2, mentions plants but not animals), CAFTA-DR (Article 15.9.2), Peru (Article 16.9.2), Panama (Article 15.9.2), Colombia (Article 16.9.2)

Intellectual Property Forms	TRIPS Provisions (1994)	General TRIPS-Plus Provisions in FTAs	Scale-down of TRIPS-Plus Standards
	(no mention), Australia (no mention), Korea (no mention)		
Copyrights			
Rights-management information	Not discussed NAFTA (no mention), Jordan (no mention)	Outlaws removal or alternation of information Chile (Article 17.5.6), Australia (Article 17.4.8), Singapore (Article 16.4.8), Morocco (Article 15.5.9), CAFTA-DR (Article 15.5.8), Bahrain (Article 14.4.8), Oman (Article 15.4.8), Peru (Article 16.7.5), Panama (Article 15.5.8), Colombia (Article 16.7.5), Korea (Article 18.4.8)	
Term of protection	No less than 50 years from authorized publication (Article 12) NAFTA (Article 1705.4), Jordan (no mention)	No less than 70 years from death of author or authorized publication Chile (Article 17.5.4), Singapore (Article 16.4.4), Australia (Article 17.4.4), Morocco (Article 15.5.5), CAFTA-DR (Article 15.5.4), Bahrain (Article 14.4.4), Oman (Article 15.4.4), Peru (Article 16.5.5), Panama (Article 15.5.4), Colombia (Article 16.5.5), Korea (Article 18.4.4)	
Circumvention of copyrighted work	Not discussed NAFTA (no mention)	Signatories must agree to prohibit circumvention Jordan (Article 4.6), Chile (Article 17.5.5), Singapore (Article 16.4.7), Australia (Article 17.4.7), Morocco (Article 15.5.8), CAFTA-DR (Article 15.5.7), Bahrain (Article 14.4.7), Oman (Article 15.4.7), Peru (Article 16.7.4), Panama (Article 15.5.7), Colombia (Article 16.7.4), Korea (Article 18.4.7)	
ISP Liability	Not discussed NAFTA (no mention), Jordan (no mention)	ISPs are provided with limited liability in certain situations of copyright infringement on their servers if they comply with regulations Chile (Article 17.11.23), Singapore (Article 16.9.22), Australia (Article 17.11.29), Morocco, CAFTA-DR (Article 15.11.27), Bahrain, Oman (Article 15.10.29), Peru (Article 16.11.29), Panama (Article 15.11.27), Colombia (Article 16.11.29), Korea (Article 18.10.30)	

Source: CRS Analysis of FTA provisions.

Note: When there is no mention of an issue in an FTA, the TRIPS standard generally holds.

APPENDIX C. OVERVIEW OF IPR-RELATED U.S. GOVERNMENT AGENCIES AND COORDINATING BODIES

What follows is a discussion of key U.S. government agencies and coordinating bodies involved in U.S. efforts to protect and enforce IPR.

Office of the United States Trade Representative (USTR)

The USTR is the lead U.S. trade negotiator and negotiates IPR provisions in U.S. trade agreements, at the multilateral, plurilateral, regional, and bilateral levels. Currently, the USTR is negotiating the proposed TPP and TTIP agreements.[89] It also enforces U.S. rights under existing trade agreements. Additionally, through its annual *Special 301 Report*, USTR is charged with monitoring the adequacy and effectiveness of IPR protection of our trading partners as well as their compliance with bilateral and multilateral trade agreements, to identify countries not in compliance with such agreements, and to negotiate with those countries better compliance. The USTR further administers the GSP program, under which a country's eligibility for U.S. trade preferences may be contingent on its IPR protection.

Department of Commerce (Commerce)

Two agencies within the Department of Commerce, the Patent and Trademark Office and the International Trade Administration, address IPR issues.[90]

- The **Patent and Trademark Office (PTO)** administers the U.S. laws pertaining to patents and trademarks. It processes patent and trademark applications, and issues patents and registers trademarks. The PTO develops IPR protection and enforcement policy and collaborates with other agencies to develop intellectual property provisions in FTAs and other international agreements. Additionally, the PTO offers training, technical assistance, and trade capacity building programs to assist in promoting strong IPR regimes in foreign countries.[91] Its IPR Attaché Program places individuals with technical expertise and experience overseas to promote strong international IPR protection and enforcement, such as through helping to influence laws, regulations, and practices in host countries. The PTO does not have jurisdiction over determining patent and trademark infringements; such determinations and remedies are made at the U.S. federal district court level or through the U.S. International Trade Commission's section 337 proceedings (discussed above). The PTO is fully funded through fees generated from patent and trademark applications.

- The **International Trade Administration (ITA)** administers many of the international trade programs of the Department of Commerce, include aspects involving IPR. The ITA monitors foreign countries' progress in implementing intellectual property agreements; reviews Generalized System of Preferences (GSP) petitions submitted by industry and coordinates the Commerce Department's response to these petitions; represents the Commerce Department at the WTO TRIPS Council; meets with trading partners to advance U.S. intellectual property interests abroad; and works with U.S. businesses and industry groups to make sure that IPR-related trade concerns are addressed.[92]

Department of Justice (DOJ)

The DOJ enforces criminal laws that protect IPR in the United States and internationally through the prosecution of intellectual property cases. Key units of the DOJ that have IPR enforcement responsibilities are the Criminal Division, U.S. Attorney's Office, the Civil Division, the Federal Bureau of Investigation, and the Office of Justice Programs.

- The **Criminal Division** prosecutes intellectual property crimes involving criminal offenses, namely through its Computer Crime and Intellectual Property Section (CCIPS).
- Federal prosecutors in the **U.S. Attorneys' Offices** pursue computer crime and intellectual property offenses.
- The **Federal Bureau of Investigation (FBI)** has an intellectual property enforcement program focusing on intellectual property crimes that have the most bearing on national and economic security, such as trade secret theft, Internet priority, and counterfeit tracking goods. Its IPR mission is to "disrupt and dismantle state sponsored

groups and international and domestic criminal organizations that steal, manufacture, distribute and otherwise profit from the theft of intellectual property." IPR is a top priority of the cyber division, though IPR crimes may be investigated in other divisions. Other IPR priorities for investigations are counterfeit health and safety products and theft of trade secrets.

- The **Civil Division** prosecutes civil actions to recover penalties imposed by the Department of Homeland Security's Customs and Border Protection (CBP, discussed below) with respect to importation of counterfeit goods, brings affirmative cases when U.S. intellectual property rights are infringed, and defends CBP enforcement of the International Trade Commission's Section 337 exclusion orders, among other things.
- The **Office of Justice Program** awards grants to support intellectual property enforcement efforts by state and local law enforcement partners.

In addition to enforcement activities, the DOJ also works with Congress to develop laws that increase protection of IPR and provides training and technical assistance programs on IPR enforcement through its Criminal Division.

Department of Homeland Security (DHS)

One of the aims of DHS is to ensure the facilitation of legitimate trade, while enforcing U.S. trade and IPR laws and investigating IPR violations, specifically trademark, counterfeiting, and copyright piracy. Key parts of DHS that are involved in IPR enforcement include U.S. Customs and Border Protection, U.S. Immigration and Customs Enforcement, U.S. Secret Service (USSS), and the National Intellectual Property Rights Coordination Center.

- Taking the lead in day-to-day IPR enforcement activities at the U.S. border, the **Customs and Border Protection (CBP)** is responsible for detecting and seizing counterfeit and pirated goods entering the United States and determining penalties for infringement.[93] CBP has the authority to determine whether or not imports infringe federally registered trademarks and copyrights and to detain or seize such infringing goods. Owners of copyrights and trademarks are able to record information about their rights in the CBP's electronic IPR database. As noted earlier, in contrast to trademarks and copyrights, CBP does not have the jurisdiction to make determinations about patent infringements. However, it is able to block imports determined by the ITC to infringe a U.S. patent by a Section 337 investigation.[94]

- **Immigration and Customs Enforcement (ICE)** is charged with investigating violations of U.S. law that are connected with U.S. borders. ICE identifies, investigates, apprehends, and removes international criminal groups and other criminals. ICE conducts inquiries into the importation and distribution of counterfeit goods. ICE activities are closely linked with those of CBP. For instance, when CBP identifies and seizes counterfeit goods, the issue is referred to ICE for criminal investigation. Likewise, information obtained from ICE that is relevant to identifying and apprehending counterfeit shipments is provided to CBP.
- The **U.S. Secret Service (USSS)** investigates violations of laws relating to counterfeiting of obligations and securities of the United States; financial crimes; and computer-based attacks on U.S. financial, banking, telecommunications, and other critical infrastructure. As part of such activities, USSS may find links to IPR violations.

Department of Health and Human Services

The FDA, which is an agency of the Department of Health and Human Services (DHHS), is responsible for protecting public health by ensuring the safety and effectiveness of medicines, food, and other products. As part of its activities, the FDA works to protect consumers against counterfeit medicines. To combat the entry of foreign counterfeit drugs into the U.S. drug supply, the FDA works in conjunction with the CBP to conduct border inspections of FDA-regulated products. The FDA also engages in foreign inspections to ensure that foreign manufacturers meet FDA quality and labeling requirements. Funding for preventing counterfeits from entering the United States is part of overall FDA import safety efforts.[95]

Library of Congress

The Copyright Office of the Library of Congress administers U.S. copyright law by registering claims to copyright and related documents, including "assignments or transfers of rights" and maintains information on registrations, recordings, compulsory licenses, and other copyright-related actions. Additionally, the Copyright Office provides legal and technical expertise on national and international copyright issues to the U.S. government. The Copyright Office also works with other federal agencies to provide assistance and advice in negotiations for international intellectual property agreements, as well as technical assistance to foreign countries crafting their own copyright laws.[96]

Department of State

The Department of State represents U.S. views in both bilateral and multilateral arenas. It works to build international consensus for IPR enforcement. Information from State's foreign postings informs the USTR Special 301 review. In particular, the Bureau of International Narcotics Control and Law Enforcement (INCLE) works to combat intellectual property piracy, while the Bureau of Economics and Business Affairs supports stronger international IPR standards to combat global piracy and counterfeiting.[97]

U.S. Agency for International Development (AID)

AID funds training and technical assistance to improve the compliance with the TRIPS Agreement and bilateral trade agreements with the United States. Funding for these projects generally have been undertaken by regional or country missions; there is no separate budgetary line item for IPR enforcement and training.[98]

United States International Trade Commission (ITC)

The ITC is a quasi-judicial federal government agency responsible for investigating and arbitrating complaints of unfair trade practices. The ITC adjudicates allegations of imported products that infringe U.S. patents, trademarks, and copyrights through its section 337 proceedings (see above). The primary remedy employed by the ITC is to order the CBP to stop imports from entering the border. Additionally, the ITC may issue "cease and desist" orders against individuals determined to be IPR violators. Damages for IPR infringement cannot be received through ITC court proceedings; right holders seeking damages must file a civil action with a U.S. federal district court.[99]

Coordinating and Advisory Bodies

The USTR leads interagency coordination of U.S. trade policy formulation, negotiation, and implementation. Beyond this general mechanism, the U.S. government also has interagency intended to specifically coordinate IPR protection and enforcement activities, as well as private sector advisory bodies that provide input into the formulation of U.S trade policy. Certain key coordinating and advisory bodies are outlined below.

Office of the U.S. Intellectual Property Enforcement Coordinator (IPEC)

The IPEC, located in the Office of Management and Budget (OMB) of the Executive Office of the President, provides executive direction and coordination of federal agencies involved in IPR enforcement. The position of the U.S. Intellectual Property Enforcement Coordinator, subject to Senate confirmation, was statutorily established in October 2008, through the Prioritizing Resources and Organization for Intellectual Property Act of 2008 (P.L. 110-403).[100] Among its key responsibilities are to develop and implement a "Joint Strategic Plan on Intellectual Property Enforcement" for combating counterfeiting and piracy (see **text box**); provide assistance to the USTR in conducting trade negotiations relating to IPR enforcement abroad; and chair an Advisory Committee composed of representatives from the OMB; Departments of Justice, Commerce, State, Homeland Security, Agriculture; FDA; AID; and the Register of Copyrights.

National Intellectual Property Rights Coordination Center (NIPRCC)

The Department of Homeland Security houses the NIPRCC, a task force for optimizing the roles and law enforcement of member agencies and enhancing government-industry partnerships to support IPR enforcement initiatives. NIPRCC is run jointly by ICE and the FBI. According to USTR, NIPRCC can be distinguished from ITEC because of the former's focus on the law enforcement response to IPR theft (primarily coordinating investigation and prosecution of IPR infringers under U.S. criminal laws) and the latter's focus on enforcement of U.S. rights under trade agreements across a range of issues, one of which is IPR.[101]

Interagency Trade Enforcement Center (ITEC)

The ITEC is an interagency coordinating body established in February 28, 2012, by Executive Order. Its aim is to strengthen and coordinate enforcement of U.S. rights under international free trade agreements and of U.S. trade laws.[102] The ITEC is housed within the USTR with a designated director from the USTR; a designated deputy director from the Department of Commerce; and support from the Departments of State, the Treasury, Justice, Agriculture, Commerce, and Homeland Security, as well as the Director of National Intelligence. The Administration has emphasized the need for creating the ITEC in order to better combat unfair trade practices by countries such as China. According to USTR, the creation of ITEC will double the resources to bring trade dispute resolution cases at the WTO "more effectively and more swiftly."[103]

Private Sector Advisory Committee System

The USTR manages a private sector advisory committee system for trade policy, intended to provide information and advisory on U.S. negotiating objectives and bargaining positions before the United States enters into trade agreements, the operation of existing U.S. trade agreements, and other U.S. trade policy matters.[104] Statutorily established under section 135 of the Trade Act of 1974 (P.L. 93-618), the private sector advisory system includes 16 Industry Trade Advisory Committees (ITACs), which are jointly administered by the USTR and Department of Commerce. ITAC membership draws from industry and labor. The ITACs reflect a range of U.S. economic sectors and policy issues, and one of the ITACs focuses on IPR.[105]

End Notes

[1] *U.S. Constitution*, Article 1, Section 8.

[2] In some cases, the effective duration of patent protection can be shorter, for example, because of regulatory delays in the approval of the patent or delays in obtaining marketing approval for the patented invention.

[3] Uniform Trade Secret Act, §1(4).

[4] Counterfeit goods should be distinguished from generic goods, i.e., in the case of generic forms of pharmaceutical medicines.

[5] National Science Board (NSB), *Science and Engineering Indicators 2012*, Arlington, VA, 2012, pp. 6-8.

[6] The NSB notes the following caveat from W. Cohen, R. Nelson, and J. Walsh, "Protecting Their Intellectual Assets: Appropriability Conditions and Why U.S. Manufacturing Firms Patent (or Not)," National Bureau of Economic Research (NBER), Working Paper No. 7552, 2000: Patenting is an intermediate step toward innovation, and patent data provide indirect and partial indicators of innovation. Not all inventions are patented, and the propensity to patent differs by industry and technology. Not all patents are of equal value, and not all foster innovation—patents may be obtained to block rivals, negotiate with competitors help in infringement lawsuits.

[7] WIPO, "Strong Growth in Demand for Intellectual Property Rights in 2012," press release, March 19, 2013, http://www.wipo.int/pressroom/en/articles/2013/article_0006.html.

[8] Stephen E. Siwek, "Engines of Growth: Economic Contributions of the US Intellectual Property Industries," commissioned by NBC Universal, 2005, p. 2.

[9] Department of Commerce, *Intellectual Property and the U.S. Economy: Industries in Focus*, March 2012, http://www.uspto.gov/news/publications/IP_Report_March_2012.pdf.

[10] It is important to note that trade statistics may not capture the full importance of intellectual property (IP)-intensive products to the U.S. economy, as many IP-intensive products are manufactured abroad as part of the global supply chain, and the full value added of these products is not accounted for in trade statistics. In addition, services statistics are limited.

[11] CRS Report R43291, *U.S. Foreign Trade in Services: Trends and U.S. Policy Challenges*, by William H. Cooper.

[12] CRS analysis of data from BEA, U.S. International Services data.

[13] Stephen E. Siwek, *Copyright Industries in the U.S. Economy: The 2013 Report*, Economists Incorporated, Prepared for the International Intellectual Property Alliance (IIPA), http://www.iipa.com/pdf/ 2013_Copyright_Industries_Full_Report.PDF.

[14] PhRMA, *2013 Biopharmaceutical Research Industry Profile*, Washington, DC, July 2013, http://www.phrma.org/ sites/default/files/pdf/PhRMA%20Profile%202013.pdf.

[15] Thomas Rogers and Andrew Zamosszegi, *Fair Use in the U.S. Economy: Economic Contribution of Industries Relying on Fair Use*, Prepared for the Computer & Communications Industry Association (CCIA), 2010. CCIA, "Fair Use Doctrine Vital for All of Us," press release, November 18, 2009, http://www.ccianet.org/index.asp? sid=5&artid= 125&evtflg=False. See also CRS Report RL33631, *Copyright Licensing in Music Distribution, Reproduction, and Public Performance*, by Brian T. Yeh.

[16] PhRMA, *2013 Biopharmaceutical Research Industry Profile.*

[17] For example, see Global Intellectual Property Center (GIPC), U.S. Chamber of Commerce, *Measuring Momentum: GIPC International IP Index*, First Edition, December 2012, http://www.theglobalipcenter.com/measuring-momentumthe-gipc-international-ip-index/.

[18] National Intellectual Property Rights Coordination Center, *Intellectual Property Rights Violations: A Report on Threats to United States Interests at Home and Abroad*, November 2011 (hereinafter, NIPRCC, 2011).

[19] Robert G. Picard, "A Note on Economic Losses Due to Theft, Infringement, and Piracy of Protected Works," *Journal of Media Economics*, 17(3), 207-217, 2004.

[20] Envisional, *Technical Report: An Estimate of Infringing Use of the Internet*, January 2011.

[21] U.S. Government Accountability Office (GAO), *Intellectual Property: Observations on Efforts to Quantify the Economic Effects of Counterfeit and Pirated Goods*, GAO-10-423, April 2010; and Commission on the Theft of American Intellectual Property, *The IP Commission Report*.

[22] NIPRCC, 2011.

[23] OECD, *The Economic Impact of Counterfeiting and Piracy*, June 2008, http://www.oecd.org/fr/sti/ind/ theeconomicimpactofcounterfeitingandpiracy.htm.

[24] OECD, *Magnitude of Counterfeiting and Piracy of Tangible Products: An Update*, November 2009.

[25] Frontier Economics, *Estimating the Global Economic and Social Impacts of Counterfeiting and Piracy*, A Report Commissioned by Business Action to Stop Counterfeiting and Piracy (BASCAP), February 2011.

[26] Ibid.

[27] Department of Homeland Security (DHS), *Intellectual Property Rights: Fiscal Year 2012 Seizure Statistics*, Prepared by U.S. Customs and Border Protection (CBP), Office of International Trade, http://www.cbp.gov/linkhandler/cgov/ trade/priority_trade/ipr/ipr_ communications/seizure/fy2012_final_stats.ctt/fy2012_final_stats.pdf.

[28] Ibid.http://www.cbp.gov/linkhandler/cgov/trade/priority_trade/ipr/ipr_communications /seizure /fy2012_final_stats.ctt/fy2012_final_stats.pdf

[29] Ibid.

[30] There may be limitations on data estimating the impact of counterfeiting and piracy on the U.S. economy. Some critics point out that many of the estimates for losses associated with IPR infringement are generated by industry groups that may have self-interested motivations.

[31] Commission on the Theft of American Intellectual Property, *The IP Commission Report*.

[32] The GATT was originally established in 1947.

[33] USTR, "United States Files WTO Cases Against China Over Deficiencies in China's Intellectual Property Rights Laws and Market Access Barriers to Copyright-Based Industries," press release, April 9, 2007, http://www.ustr.gov. See also CRS Report RL33536, *China-U.S. Trade Issues*, by Wayne M. Morrison.

[34] WTO, "WTO issues panel report on U.S.-China dispute over intellectual property rights," press release, January 26, 2009. USTR, "United States Wins WTO Dispute Over Deficiencies in China's Intellectual Property Rights Law," press release, January 26, 2009. Daniel Pruzin, "WTO Publishes Final Ruling in U.S. Complaint Against Chinese IPR Enforcement Measures," *International Trade Daily*, January 27, 2009.

[35] See CRS Report RL33536, *China-U.S. Trade Issues*, by Wayne M. Morrison.

[36] Pascal Lamy, "Trade-Related Aspects of Intellectual Property Rights - Ten Years Later," *Journal of World Trade,* October 2004, p. 925.

[37] "Extension of the Transition Period under Article 66.1 of the TRIPS Agreement for Least-Developed Country Members for Certain Obligations with Respect to Pharmaceutical Products," WTO Document IP/C/25, July 1, 2002.

[38] WTO TRIPS Council, "Extension of the Transition Period Under Article 66.1 for Least Developed Country Members," June 12, 2013.

[39] Declaration on the TRIPS Agreement and Public Health, (WT/MIN(01)/DEC/2), November 14, 2001, available at http://www.wto.org/english/thewto_e/minist_e/min01_e/mindecl_ trips_e.htm.

[40] Compulsory licenses are issued by governments to authorize the use of or production of a patented item by a domestic party other than a patent holder.

[41] OECD, *The Impact of Trade-Related Intellectual Property Rights on Trade and Foreign Direct Investment in Developing Countries*, May 28, 2003, p. 21, http://www.oecd.org.

[42] Keith E. Maskus, *Intellectual Property Rights in the Global Economy*, Institute for International Economics (IIE), Washington, D.C., August 2000.

[43] Commission on Intellectual Property Rights (CIPR), *Integrating Intellectual Property Rights and Development Policy*, September 2002.

[44] "Implementation of Paragraph 6 of the Doha Declaration on the TRIPS Agreement and Public Health," IP/C/W/405, August 30, 2003, and accompanying Chairman's statement, available at http://www.wto.org/english/news_e/pres03_e/ pr350_e.htm.

[45] WTO, "Intellectual property meeting mulls Irish tobacco plan, drug tariffs, sport, non-violation, press release, October 10 and 11, 2013.

[46] "Members accepting amendment of the TRIPS Agreement," http://www.wto.org/english /tratop_e/trips_e/ amendment_e.htm.

[47] "Canada Issues Compulsory License For HIV/AIDS Drug Export To Rwanda, In First Test Of WTO Procedure," *Bridges Weekly Trade News Digest*, September 26, 2007, http://www.ictsd.org/weekly/07-09-26/story2.htm.

[48] These WCT and WPPT frequently are referred to as the WIPO Internet Treaties.

[49] Monika Ermert, "G8 Governments Want ACTA Finalised This Year, SPLT Talks Accelerated," *Intellectual Property Watch*, July 9, 2008.

[50] WIPO, "Standing Committee on the Law of Patents (SCP)," http://www.wipo.int /policy

[51] See CRS Report RL33743, *Trade Promotion Authority (TPA) and the Role of Congress in Trade Policy*, by William H. Cooper.

[52] P.L. 107-210, Sec. 2102(b)(4).

[53] The May 10, 2007, bipartisan trade agreement is available online at http://www.ustr.gov/assets Fact_Sheets/2007/asset_upload_file127_11319.pdf.

[54] See CRS Report R42694, *The Trans-Pacific Partnership (TPP) Negotiations and Issues for Congress*, coordinated by Ian F. Fergusson.

[55] USTR Blog Post, November 29, 2013, http://www.ustr.gov/about-us/press-office/blog/2013 /November/stakeholderinput-sharpens-focuses-us-work-on-pharmaceutical

[56] Henry Farrell, "Five Key Questions – and Answers- About the Leaked TPP Text," *Washington Post* Blog, November 15, 2013 http://www.washingtonpost.com/blogs/ and Electronic Frontier Foundation, "TPP Leak Confirms the Worst: U.S. Negotiators Still Trying to Trade Away Internet Freedoms," https://www.eff.org/deeplinks/2013/11/tpp-leak-confirms-worst-us-negotiatorsstill-trying-trade

[57] See CRS Report R43158, *Proposed Transatlantic Trade and Investment Partnership (TTIP): In Brief*, by Shayerah Ilias Akhtar and Vivian C. Jones.

[58] U.S.-EU High Level Working Group on Jobs and Growth, *Final Report of the U.S.-EU High Level Working Group on Jobs and Growth*, February 11, 2013, http://www.ustr.gov/about-us/press-office/reports-and-publications/2013/ final-report-us-eu-hlwg.

[59] USTR, *2012 National Trade Estimate Report on Foreign Trade Barriers*, p. 148, http://www.ustr.gov/about-us/ press-office/reports-and-publications/2012-1.

[60] Executive Office of the President, *Administration's Strategy on Mitigating the Theft of U.S. Trade Secrets*, February 2013, http://www.whitehouse.gov//sites/default/files/omb/IPEC/ admin_strategy_on_mitigating_the_theft_of_u.s._trade_secrets.pdf.

[61] For a more detailed discussion of the differences between the TRIPS Agreement and regional FTAs that are in force, see CRS Report RL33205, *Intellectual Property and the Free Trade Agreements: Innovation Policy Issues*, by John R. Thomas.

[62] "Brand-Name Industry Alarmed at IPR Precedent of FTA Template," *Inside US Trade*, May 18, 2007.

[63] While TRIPS does not directly speak to the rights of generic drug manufacturers in obtaining marketing approval for a generic drug before the expiration of the patented drug, Article 30

of TRIPS permits exceptions of patent rights for activities such as "research, prior user rights, and pre-expiration testing."

[64] For example, under the Peru FTA, if a company files to market a new drug in Peru after making an initial filing in another country, such as the United States, and Peru approves the drug within six months of the filing, the data exclusivity period begins at the time the drug was approved in the country of the initial filing, not Peru.

[65] U.S. Government Accountability Office, *U.S. Trade Policy Guidance on WTO Declaration on Access to Medicines May Need Clarification*, GAO-97-1198, September 2007, p. 19.

[66] CRS Report RL33205, *Intellectual Property and the Free Trade Agreements: Innovation Policy Issues*, by John R. Thomas.

[67] The DMCA (P.L. 105-304) prohibits disabling technological protection measures designed to protect copyright works through activities such as descrambling or decrypting copyrighted works.

[68] For more information on U.S. trade secret law, see CRS Report R41391, *The Role of Trade Secrets in Innovation Policy*, by John R. Thomas.

[69] Executive Office of the President, *Administration Strategy on Mitigating the Theft of U.S. Trade Secrets*, February 2013, p. 4.

[70] The term "indigenous innovation" can be tied to China's Medium- to Long-term Plan for the Development of Science and Technology, released in January 26, which calls for China to become an "innovation-oriented society" and a global leader in science and technology.

[71] U.S. International Trade Commission, *China: Effects of Intellectual Property Infringement and Indigenous Innovation Policies on the U.S. Economy*, Investigation No. 332-519, USITC Publication 4226, May 2011.

[72] For more information, see CRS Report RL33536, *China-U.S. Trade Issues*, by Wayne M. Morrison.

[73] USTR, *2013 National Trade Estimate Report on Foreign Trade Barriers*, March 2013.

[74] As defined by USTR, "local content" requirements are requirements to purchase domestically-manufactured goods or domestically-supplied services.

[75] *USTR, 2013 Special 301 Report.*

[76] Amy Kazmin, "India Revokes GSK Patent for Version of Cancer Drug," *Financial Times*, August 2, 2013; Amy Kazmin, "India: Patents and Precedents," *Financial Times*, May 15, 2013.

[77] Under NAFTA, patents shall be granted "provided that such inventions are new, result from an inventive step, and are capable of industrial application." NAFTA provides that "inventive step," and "capable of industrial application," are synonymous with "non-obvious," and "useful," which underpins the concept of utility. Article 1709(1).

[78] "Canada's Internationally Inconsistent "Promise Doctrine" for Patents," Eli Lilly background document.

[79] "Canada: Eli Lilly Files Notice of Arbitration in $500 million NAFTA Dispute Against Canada," Bereskin and Parr, LLP, September 24, 2013.

[80] "The 'Promise of the Patent' in Canadian Patent Law," Heenan Blaikie, LLP, Flash Bulletin, December 2013.

[81] For the Special 301 provisions, see 19 U.S.C. §2242; Trade Act of 1974, as amended, (P.L. 93-618), §182.

[82] S. Rep. No. 93-1298, 93d Cong. 2d Sess. 199 (1974).

[83] ITC, *FY2014 Congressional Budget Justification.*

[84] See CRS Report RL33663, *Generalized System of Preferences: Background and Renewal Debate*, by Vivian C. Jones.

[85] 91 U.S.C. §2462(b)(2).

[86] USTR, *GSP: 2012 Annual Review*, http://www.ustr.gov.

[87] See CRS Report R43052, *U.S. International Investment Agreements: Issues for Congress*, by Shayerah Ilias Akhtar and Martin A. Weiss. U.S. BITs provide investment protections through provisions such as requirements for nondiscriminatory treatment, protections against expropriation, and the right to neutral, binding arbitration to resolve disputes investors and host countries.

[88] See CRS Report RL33663, *Generalized System of Preferences: Background and Renewal Debate*, by Vivian C. Jones; and Stephen Ezell, *Withdraw India's GSP Preference If It Continues to Impose Localization Barriers to Trade on Foreign Enterprises*, ITIF, January 23, 2013, http://www.innovationfiles.org/withdraw-indias-gsp-preference-if-itcontinues-to-impose-localization

[89] See CRS Report R42694, *The Trans-Pacific Partnership (TPP) Negotiations and Issues for Congress*, coordinated by Ian F. Fergusson, and CRS Report R43387, *Transatlantic Trade and Investment Partnership (TTIP) Negotiations*, by Shayerah Ilias Akhtar and Vivian C. Jones.

[90] General information about the Department of Commerce is available at http://www.doc.gov.

[91] NIPLECC, *Report to the President and Congress on Coordination of Intellectual Property Enforcement and Protection*, January 2008, p. 21.

[92] NIPLECC, *Report to the President and Congress on Coordination of Intellectual Property Enforcement and Protection*, January 2008, p. 21.

[93] Certain customs-related IPR policy-making resides within the Treasury.

[94] NIPLECC, *Report to the President and Congress on Coordination of Intellectual Property Enforcement and Protection*, January 2008, pp. 15-16. Additional information about CBP is available at http://www.cbp.gov.

[95] Conversation with FDA official, November 26, 2007. Additional information is available on the FDA website, http://www.fda.gov.

[96] NIPLECC, *Report to the President and Congress on Coordination of Intellectual Property Enforcement and Protection*, January 2008, p. 18. Also see Copyright Office website, http://www.copyright.

[97] NIPLECC, *Report to the President and Congress on Coordination of Intellectual Property Enforcement and Protection*, January 2008, pp. 17-18. Additional information about the State Department is available at http://www.state.

[98] Trade Capacity Database and general AID information is accessible at http://www.usaid.gov.

[99] ITC website, http://www.usitc.gov.

[100] In creating the IPEC, P.L. 110-403 repealed the authorities creating the National Intellectual Property Law Enforcement Coordination Council (NIPLECC). Established by Congress in 1999, NIPLECC coordinated U.S. activities to protect and enforce IPR domestically and abroad, drawing together the major federal agencies the help to enforce IPR. The Copyright Office participated in the Council in an advisory role. The U.S. Coordinator for International Intellectual Property Enforcement headed NIPLECC's interagency coordination efforts. NIPLECC, *Report to the President and Congress on Coordination of Intellectual Property Enforcement and Protection*, January 2008, pp. 3-4.

[101] USTR, "ITEC Frequently Asked Questions."

[102] The White House, Office of the Press Secretary, "Executive Order—Establishment of the Interagency Trade Enforcement Center," February 28, 2012.

[103] World Trade Online, "Trade Enforcement Unit Will Not Dilute U.S. Standard for Bringing WTO Cases," March 1, 2012.

[104] USTR, "Advisory Committees," http://www.ustr.gov/about-us/intergovernmental-affairs/advisory-committee.s

[105] USTR, "Industry Trade Advisory Committees (ITAC)," http://www.ustr.gov/about-us/advisory-committees/ industry-trade-advisory-committees-itac.

In: Intellectual Property Rights
Editor: Evelyn P. Gilbert

ISBN: 978-1-63482-396-8

Chapter 2

INTELLECTUAL PROPERTY: U.S. CUSTOMS AND BORDER PROTECTION COULD BETTER MANAGE ITS PROCESS TO ENFORCE EXCLUSION ORDERS*

United States Government Accountability Office

ABBREVIATIONS

CBP	Customs and Border Protection
CROSS	Customs Rulings Online Search System
DHS	Department of Homeland Security
IPR Branch	Intellectual Property Rights Branch
IPR-NTAG	Intellectual Property Rights National Targeting and Analysis Group
ITC	International Trade Commission
OMB	Office of Management and Budget
USTR	United States Trade Representative

* This is an edited, reformatted and augmented version of The United States Government Accountability Office publication, GAO-15-78, dated November 2014.

WHY GAO DID THIS STUDY

Under Section 337 of the Tariff Act of 1930, ITC investigates allegations of unfair import practices, including unlicensed use of intellectual property rights such as patents, copyrights, and trademarks. If ITC finds a violation of this law, it generally issues an exclusion order that directs CBP to deny entry of infringing products into U.S. commerce. CBP must determine, without inhibiting legitimate trade, whether products arriving at 328 U.S. ports are covered by exclusion orders.

GAO was asked to review CBP's enforcement of exclusion orders. This report (1) describes CBP's processes for enforcing exclusion orders and (2) assesses CBP's management of its enforcement process at ports of entry. GAO analyzed CBP and ITC documents and data from October 2009 through April 2014 and interviewed CBP and ITC officials.

WHAT GAO RECOMMENDS

GAO recommends that CBP update its internal guidance with requirements to (1) routinely ensure that trade alerts are posted to the CBP intranet for each exclusion order, (2) routinely identify any orders whose changed conditions merit a CBP request that ITC rescind them, and (3) monitor timeliness of trade alert issuance. CBP concurred with recommendations one and three and described actions planned or under way to address them. However, CBP did not concur with recommendation number two. According to CBP, it is not mandated to identify potentially outdated orders and request that ITC rescind them. GAO continues to believe the recommendation is valid for reasons discussed in the report.

WHAT GAO FOUND

The Department of Homeland Security's U.S. Customs and Border Protection (CBP) uses two processes to enforce exclusion orders issued by the U.S. International Trade Commission (ITC): a four-phase process to detect and deny entry to or seize infringing products at U.S. ports and an administrative ruling process that determines in advance of importing whether products are covered by exclusion orders. In the first phase of the process to enforce exclusion orders at the ports, CBP drafts a trade alert that provides enforcement instructions to CBP national targeting groups and local officials at all ports of entry to identify shipments for examination; without an alert, officials said, it would be difficult for CBP components to enforce an exclusion order. From September 2010 through April 2014, CBP excluded 158 shipments of products, such as ink cartridges and footwear. Before a company attempts to import a certain product, it may request that CBP determine through its administrative ruling process whether the product is covered by a particular exclusion order.

U.S. Customs and Border Protection's Process to Enforce Exclusion Orders at the Ports

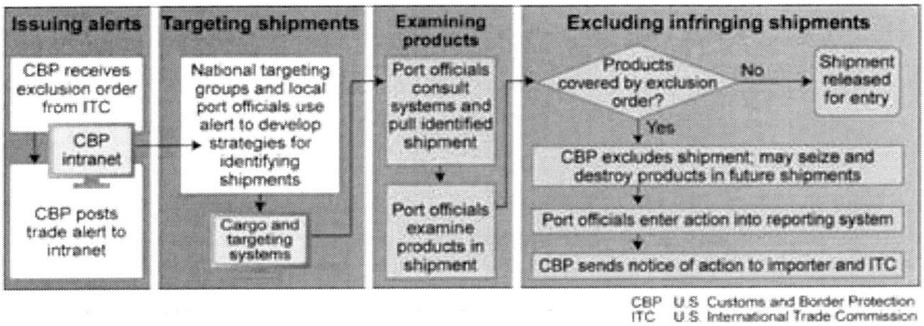

Source: GAO analysis of CBP documents and interviews with CBP officials.| GAO-15-78.

CBP's management of its exclusion order enforcement process at the ports contains weaknesses that result in inefficiencies and an increased risk of infringing products entering U.S. commerce. First, CBP does not routinely review ITC's list of exclusion orders or take other action to ensure that a trade alert has been posted to its intranet for each order. At GAO's request, CBP reviewed ITC's list of exclusion orders as of April 30, 2014, and reported that it had posted trade alerts for 83 of the 94 exclusion orders; however, it posted 17 of the 83 trade alerts after GAO's request for data. Without routinely taking action to ensure that trade alerts are posted to CBP's intranet, infringing products could enter into U.S. commerce. Second, CBP does not routinely review ITC's list of exclusion orders to identify orders that may be candidates for rescission by ITC. Requesting rescission of exclusion orders could enable CBP to focus its enforcement efforts more effectively and efficiently. Third, CBP's guidance lacks time frames for issuing trade alerts, which prevents CBP from monitoring timeliness. GAO found that it took CBP from 2 days to 3 months to request a posting of a trade alert to the intranet during the period from October 2009 through April 2014. Without actively managing trade alerts and establishing time frames for posting alerts, CBP management cannot hold staff accountable for timely enforcement of exclusion orders, and there is an increased risk of infringing products entering U.S. commerce.

* * *

November 19, 2014

The Honorable Ron Wyden
Chairman

The Honorable Orrin G. Hatch
Ranking Member
Committee on Finance
United States Senate

Intellectual property plays an important role in the U.S. economy. The nation's legal and regulatory system of intellectual property rights, according to a 2012 Department of Commerce report,[1] helps establish and sustain industries, drives innovation, and facilitates trade and commerce. Protecting intellectual property rights against infringement, however, is costly and complex. Companies may spend millions in litigation to protect their intellectual property rights, and determining whether specific imported products infringe on intellectual property rights can be complicated, particularly for technologically advanced products. Smartphones, for instance, combine software and hardware that undergo rapid changes in design and functionality. A single smartphone may have features and functions described in over 100,000 patents, including, for example, the phone's rounded corners or the particular finger movement needed to unlock the touch screen.

Under Section 337 of the Tariff Act of 1930 (hereafter referred to as Section 337), the U.S. International Trade Commission (ITC) investigates allegations of unfair import practices, including those that infringe on intellectual property rights, such as unlicensed use of patents, copyrights, and trademarks.[2] If ITC finds a violation of this law, it generally issues an exclusion order that directs the Department of Homeland Security's (DHS) U.S. Customs and Border Protection (CBP) to deny entry of infringing products into U.S. commerce.[3] To enforce exclusion orders, CBP must determine whether products arriving at 328 U.S. ports of entry fall within the scope of exclusion orders, and as part of its mission, CBP endeavors to do so without inhibiting legitimate trade. In this report, we refer to the efforts that CBP undertakes to detect imports of infringing products as CBP's enforcement process at the ports. In addition to these enforcement efforts, CBP may be asked by companies to determine, in advance of importing certain products, whether those products are covered by a particular exclusion order, for instance, when a company has redesigned an infringing product such that it no longer infringes on the intellectual property right thereby falling outside the coverage of the exclusion order. In this report, we refer to these anticipatory efforts to facilitate enforcement as CBP's administrative ruling process.[4]

You requested that we review CBP's efforts to enforce exclusion orders. In this report, we (1) examine CBP's processes for enforcing exclusion orders and (2) assess CBP's management of its enforcement process at ports of entry. In this report, we neither take a position on, nor do we address, the matters pending in ongoing litigation between Microsoft and DHS related to CBP's enforcement of an exclusion order.[5]

To examine CBP's exclusion order enforcement processes and assess CBP management of its enforcement process at the ports, we (1) reviewed relevant laws, regulations, and CBP internal guidance, such as directives and procedures, and (2) interviewed CBP officials at headquarters, the field offices, and the ports, as well as officials at ITC and the Office of Management and Budget's (OMB) Office of the Intellectual Property Enforcement Coordinator. We selected ports with experience in enforcing exclusion orders as shown by CBP exclusions data from September 16, 2010, through April 30, 2014.[6] We also selected ports where we could discuss and observe CBP's exclusion order enforcement process for shipments arriving in land, sea, and air environments. We visited the ports of Buffalo and John F. Kennedy International Airport in New York and Los Angeles/Long Beach Seaport and Los Angeles International Airport in California. To understand CBP's future exclusion order enforcement efforts, we interviewed CBP officials from the Electronics Center of Excellence and Expertise in Los Angeles, California; the Industrial and Manufacturing Materials Center of Excellence and Expertise in Buffalo, New York; and the Pharmaceuticals, Health, and Chemicals Center of Excellence and Expertise in New York, New York. The information gathered from our site visits cannot be generalized to all ports and field offices. We evaluated CBP's management of its enforcement process at the ports against requirements established by its own internal guidance and by government-wide internal control standards.[7] We reviewed all exclusion orders in effect as of April 30, 2014, and collected CBP data on internal trade alerts used for targeting shipments of potentially infringing products. We also analyzed CBP data on the number of shipments CBP excluded from entry from September 16, 2010, through April 30, 2014. Using ITC exclusion order issuance dates and CBP's data on trade alert issuance dates, we analyzed the number of workdays the CBP officials took to request a posting of trade alerts to the CBP intranet from exclusion orders issued from October 1, 2009, through April 30, 2014. To assess the reliability of the data CBP provided to us, we interviewed agency officials and reviewed information regarding the underlying data systems and the checks, controls, and reviews used to generate the data and ensure their accuracy and reliability. We found the data sufficiently reliable for our purposes. For more information about our scope and methodology, see appendix I.

We conducted this performance audit from November 2013 to November 2014 in accordance with generally accepted government auditing standards. Those standards require that we plan and perform the audit to obtain sufficient, appropriate evidence to provide a reasonable basis for our findings and conclusions based on our audit objectives. We believe that the evidence obtained provides a reasonable basis for our findings and conclusions based on our audit objectives.

BACKGROUND

CBP is responsible for enforcing exclusion orders, which ITC issues upon a final determination of a violation of Section 337 and after consideration of public interest factors enumerated in the law.[8] Unlawful activities covered by Section 337 include importing into the United States articles that infringe upon certain intellectual property rights or other unfair import practices described by Section 337.[9] According to ITC, most Section 337 investigations involve allegations of patent infringement. The ITC generally completes a Section 337 investigation within 12 to 18 months, according to ITC officials. The length of an investigation may be influenced by the number of companies alleged to be importing infringing products; the number of patent infringements, or other unfair import practices, involved in the allegations; the complexity of the technology involved; the ITC staff's workload; and other factors. The ITC's investigation process consists of the seven steps shown in figure 1 and briefly summarized below.[10]

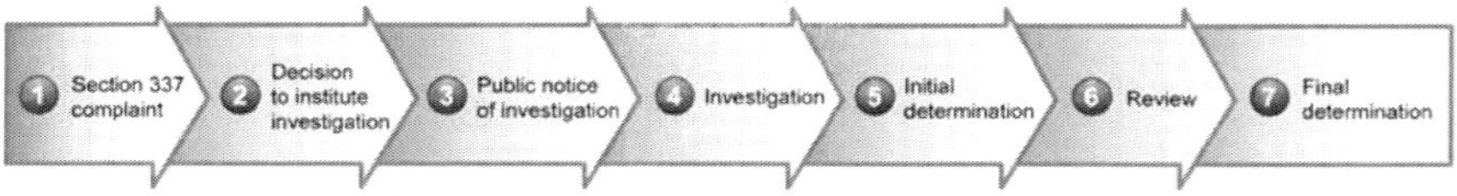

Source: GAO analysis of ITC data and interviews with officials. | GAO-15-78.

Figure 1. Summary of the U.S. International Trade Commission's Section 337 Investigation Process.

1. *Section 337 complaint:* A complainant (e.g., the intellectual property rights holder) files a complaint containing detailed facts alleging a violation of Section 337 and names the proposed respondents—the companies alleged to be involved in the manufacture, production, sale, or importation of infringing products. In response to a *Federal Register* notice published upon receipt of the complaint, the respondents and members of the public may make comments on the public interest issues arising from the complaint and potential exclusion orders. The complainant may respond to these public interest submissions.
2. *Decision to institute investigation:* The ITC's Office of Unfair Import Investigations examines the complaint for sufficiency and compliance with all ITC rules and requirements. The ITC generally makes the decision to institute an investigation within 30 to 35 days.[11]
3. *Public notice of investigation:* If the ITC determines to institute an investigation, it issues a public notice in the *Federal Register* commencing an investigation based on the complaint. The notice date establishes the official start of the Section 337 investigation. The ITC will serve a copy of the complaint and notice of the investigation to all respondents named in the investigation and to the embassies in Washington, D.C., of the foreign respondents' countries.
4. *Investigation:* The ITC delegates the investigation to the Chief Administrative Law Judge who assigns the case to an administrative law judge to preside over the proceedings. When appropriate, the Office of Unfair Import Investigations is also named as a party to the investigation. The presiding judge sets a target date by which the ITC investigation should be completed. The parties, including complainants and respondents, present information such as evidence and arguments with respect to alleged unlawful importations or sales.
5. *Initial determination:* The presiding administrative law judge holds a hearing approximately 8 to 10 months after the public notice of

investigation. After the hearing, the judge issues an initial determination as to whether the respondents violated Section 337 and, if appropriate, a recommendation for remedy (the recommended determination). The initial determination is issued no later than 4 months before the target date set by the presiding judge for completion of the investigation. The ITC invites the parties and the public to submit comments regarding the public interest considerations through a *Federal Register* notice published within 30 days of the issuance of the recommended determination.

6. *Review:* The ITC may determine to review the initial determination within 60 days of its issuance. If the ITC decides to review the initial determination, it identifies the issues under review, and requests briefings from the parties, including the complainants and respondents, on matters such as the substantive issues affecting whether there is a violation and on the remedy. The ITC also requests written submissions from the parties, other government agencies, and the public regarding remedy, bonding, and public interest.[12] At the end of the review period, the ITC issues a final decision to affirm the initial determination, modify it, reverse it, or refer the matter back to the presiding administrative law judge for further proceedings.
7. *Final determination:* The ITC publishes notice of its final determination in the *Federal Register*. If the ITC determines that there is a violation, it also determines the appropriate remedy after considering the public interest. The remedies may include an exclusion order. The ITC's determination, the resulting orders, and the record supporting its determination are transmitted to the President of the United States, the United States Trade Representative (USTR), the Secretary of the Treasury, and CBP. The exclusion order is e-mailed to CBP on the date of issuance for enforcement. [13] According to CBP officials, the ITC notifies CBP of the exclusion order by e-mail on the same day that it issues an exclusion order and thereafter meets with CBP regarding the involved exclusion order.

There are two types of exclusion orders: general and limited. General exclusion orders direct CBP to exclude all infringing products without regard to source; limited exclusion orders direct CBP to exclude infringing products from a specified company or companies. For example, a general exclusion order on infringing printer cartridges may affect all importers of printer cartridges, whereas a limited exclusion order directs CBP to exclude covered products from named respondents. Based on ITC data, there were 94 exclusion orders in effect as of April 30, 2014, about half of which were general exclusion orders that affect a greater number of companies than limited orders.

Exclusion orders cover a range of unfair acts, such as patent, trademark, and copyright infringement, as well as trade dress infringement, trade secret misappropriation, false advertising, and false designation of origin. Of the 94 exclusion orders in effect as of April 30, 2014, about 60 percent involved products such as integrated circuits, computer components, consumer electronics products, and chemical compositions that infringe U.S. patents. The 94 exclusion orders covered a range of products, such as electronic goods; machinery parts; plastic plates, lids, footwear, and toys; motor vehicle parts and accessories; energy drinks; and cigarettes. Of the 94 exclusion orders, more than half were issued in 2005 through 2014; the oldest was issued in 1979. Exclusion orders can be active until the protected intellectual property rights expire or ITC rescinds the orders.[14] See figure 2 for an overview of exclusion order characteristics.

Definitions of Patents, Trademarks, and Copyrights according to the U.S. Patent and Trademark Office

A patent is an intellectual property right granted by the government of the United States of America to an inventor "to exclude others from making, using, offering for sale, or selling the invention throughout the United States or importing the invention into the United States" for a limited time in exchange for public disclosure of the invention when the patent is granted.

A trademark is a brand name or service mark that includes any word, name, symbol, device, or any combination, used or intended to be used to identify and distinguish the goods/services of one seller or provider from those of others, and to indicate the source of the goods/services.

A copyright protects original works of authorship, such as writings, music, and works of art that have been tangibly expressed.

Source: U.S. Patent and Trademark Office | GAO-15-78.

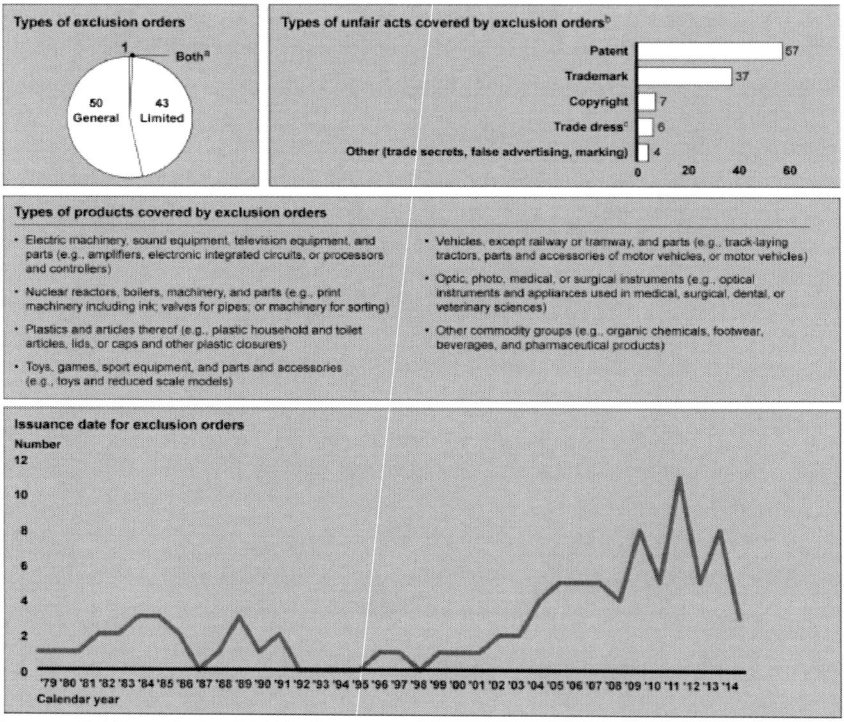

Source: GAO analysis of U.S. Customs and Border Protection and U.S. International Trade Commission data. | GAO-15-78.

[a] U.S. International Trade Commission (ITC) Investigation Number 337-TA-487 resulted in both a limited exclusion order and a general exclusion order, but it is enforced by U.S. Customs and Border Protection as a single exclusion order.

[b] The types of unfair acts listed do not total 94 because some exclusion orders may cover multiple intellectual property rights. For example, Investigation Number 337-TA-780 covers a utility patent, a design patent, and a trademark.

[c] According to ITC, trade dress is a product's total appearance and image, including features such as size, texture, shape, colors, and graphics.

Figure 2. Exclusion Orders: Types, Unfair Acts Covered, Product Categories, and Issuance Dates of Exclusion Orders in Effect as of April 30, 2014.

CBP Uses Two Processes to Enforce Exclusion Orders, Depending on Whether Products Have Already Been Shipped

CBP uses two processes to enforce exclusion orders: a four-phase process to detect and deny entry to or seize infringing products at U.S. ports and an administrative ruling process that determines in advance of importing whether products are covered by exclusion orders. Enforcement efforts begin when CBP receives the exclusion order from the ITC.[15] CBP's Office of International Trade and Office of Field Operations administer a process for enforcing exclusion orders at the ports that involves four phases: issuing trade alerts, targeting shipments, examining products, and excluding infringing shipments. CBP's Intellectual Property Rights (IPR) Branch within the Office of International Trade uses an administrative ruling process that upon request, determines in advance of importing whether products are covered by exclusion orders. (See app. II for an organization chart showing the CBP offices involved in the enforcement processes.) Companies with existing products or companies that have redesigned products such that they no longer infringe on the intellectual property rights, thereby falling outside the coverage of the exclusion order, may request that CBP determine through its administrative ruling process whether the companies can import the specified products without violating the order. CBP officials said that these companies generally submit their requests for an administrative ruling around the time when the exclusion order is issued.

CBP Uses a Four-Phase Process to Enforce Exclusion Orders at the Ports

As shown in figure 3, CBP's process to enforce exclusion orders at the ports has four phases. In the first phase, upon receiving an exclusion order from ITC, CBP drafts a trade alert that provides enforcement instructions to CBP national targeting groups and officials at all ports of entry.[16] IPR Branch officials said the trade alert generally triggers CBP's enforcement at the ports; without an alert, officials said, it would be difficult for CBP components to enforce an exclusion order. In the second phase, the national targeting groups and local port officials may develop targeting strategies for each exclusion order to detect shipments with potentially infringing products for examination.

In the third phase, port officials examine targeted shipments to determine whether the products are covered by exclusion orders. Lastly, port officials exclude or seize shipments with infringing products, notify importers and ITC of exclusions, and document exclusions in a CBP tracking system.

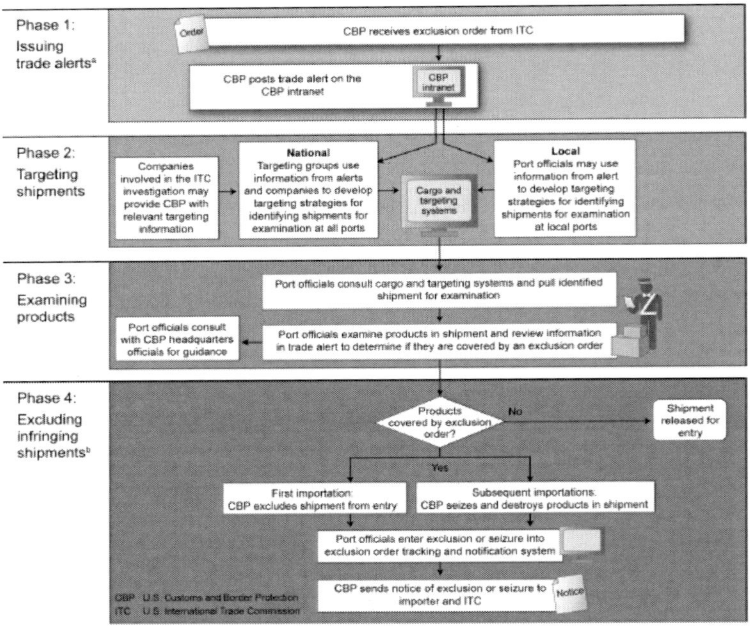

Source: GAO analysis of CBP documents and interviews with CBP efforts. | GAO-15-78.

[a] CBP officials said that companies interested in determining whether their existing or redesigned products are covered by exclusion orders generally submit their requests for an administrative ruling around the time that CBP receives notice of the exclusion order from ITC. See the discussion of CBP's administrative ruling process later in this section.

[b] After an importer's first excluded shipment, ITC generally will issue a seizure and forfeiture order to CBP, which directs CBP to seize, rather than merely deny entry to, any future shipments of the same infringing products from the importer.

Notes: Not shown in the graphic is CBP's exclusion order enforcement process during the United States Trade Representative's 60-day review period. During this review period, companies are allowed to continue importing if they secure a bond in advance of importing products, assuming a bond is required.

Figure 3. U.S. Customs and Border Protection's Process to Enforce Exclusion Orders at the Ports.

Phase 1: Issuing Trade Alerts

Using information from the exclusion order, IPR Branch officials, sometimes with assistance from CBP's Electronics Center of Excellence and Expertise (Electronics Center),[17] draft trade alerts with enforcement instructions to national targeting groups and local port officials. The trade alert generally includes information such as a description of the protected intellectual property right, names of the companies known to import infringing products, specific enforcement instructions, and the CBP national groups responsible for targeting shipments. According to standard operating procedures, IPR Branch officials post the trade alert on the CBP intranet, an internal network that officials said is accessible to all CBP officials. Upon receipt of any additional information from the ITC or the complainants,[18] the IPR Branch updates trade alerts as necessary. IPR Branch officials told us that the trade alert generally triggers CBP's enforcement at the ports; without an alert, officials said, it would be difficult for all CBP components to enforce an exclusion order.

Phase 2: Targeting Shipments

The second phase of CBP's enforcement process involves the development of national and local targeting strategies to help identify shipments with products covered by exclusion orders for possible examination.

National targeting: At the national level, the Intellectual Property Rights National Targeting and Analysis Group (IPR-NTAG) or the Electronics Center develops targeting strategies for identifying shipments with products covered by exclusion orders. Using information found in the trade alerts and other sources, officials from these groups analyze data on countries of origin, ports of entry, transportation modes, importers, shippers, and manufacturers to develop strategies. According to Electronics Center officials, information from meetings with complainants and respondents may help inform the development of their targeting strategies.

To carry out national targeting strategies, IPR-NTAG and Electronics Center officials primarily use two targeting methods: user-defined rules and cargo hold requests.

- *User-defined rules:* Based on their analysis, officials may create a user-defined rule, which is a set of criteria that is entered into CBP's national targeting system.[19] If an incoming shipment meets the criteria established in the rule, the system will identify the shipment for potential examination. User-defined rules provide continuous targeting of shipments arriving at all ports for as long as the rule exists in the system. IPR-NTAG officials said they generally test a rule for 1 to 2 weeks to determine the number of shipments identified for examination and, of those shipments examined, the number found not to contain infringing products (negative exams). Based on the resulting proportion of negative exams, officials will adjust the rule to avoid overtargeting and ensure that the number of shipments identified by the rule does not inhibit the flow of legitimate trade. Officials said that targeting with user-defined rules is straightforward for limited exclusion orders because these identify infringing importers and may also specify the shipments' countries of origin and ports of entry. For example, officials developed a user-defined rule for a limited exclusion order covering certain digital televisions; the exclusion order listed the companies known to import infringing products. By contrast, officials said that national targeting with user-defined rules may not be feasible for general exclusion orders because these are broadly scoped and user-defined rules can only be refined up to a point. General exclusion orders tend to cover products that fall under a general description, such as rubber-soled shoes, with a large volume of shipments and from multiple companies and countries of origin. As a result, user-defined rules for some general exclusion orders would identify hundreds of shipments for examination at multiple ports, resulting in numerous negative exams, thus inhibiting the flow of legitimate trade.

Officials said that user-defined rules are revised based on targeting results and any new information from complainants and respondents. If user-defined rules do not result in the detection of infringing shipments over time, officials will terminate them. However, targeting officials may create a new user-defined rule if a complainant reports to the IPR Branch that it is finding products within U.S. commerce that should have been excluded, or if a complainant gains new information on companies that are importing infringing shipments.

- *Cargo hold requests:* Officials said that if they cannot create user-defined rules, as in the case of a general exclusion order, they may manually review the information in their cargo and targeting systems and identify incoming shipments for examination based on information in the trade alert.[20] When they identify such shipments, officials send cargo hold requests to specific ports designating the shipments to be pulled for examination. These cargo hold requests may provide information such as the relevant exclusion order; a link to the trade alert; examination instructions; information relating to the importer, manufacturer, or products; and contact information for any necessary follow-up communication with the targeting groups.

Unlike user-defined rules, cargo hold requests apply only to shipments at specific ports and occur only when officials conduct manual reviews of information on arriving shipments. IPR-NTAG officials said they review information on incoming shipments as part of their regular job duties, but they noted that exclusion order enforcement is one of many enforcement activities they must conduct.[21] As a result, these officials said the number of cargo holds requested varies based on how individual officials prioritize their responsibilities to manage their workloads.

Local Operation: Interlocking Laminate Flooring

From March to May 2014, U.S. Customs and Border Protection (CBP) officials at the Port of Los Angeles/Long Beach said they conducted an operation targeting shipments of interlocking laminate flooring, which is covered by a general exclusion order. Based on their research, officials had found that 70 percent of the companies importing infringing products imported them through this port. Port officials said they targeted 58 shipments; 26 of the 58 shipments, or 45 percent, contained products that were covered by the exclusion order. As a result of the operation, officials said that the importers began sourcing their shipments from licensed manufacturers to comply with the exclusion order.

Source: CBP. | GAO-15-78.

Local targeting: Local port officials may conduct local targeting for exclusion orders when resources are available and such targeting would not duplicate national targeting efforts. Port officials told us they specialize in the commodities that commonly arrive at their ports and use their expertise to analyze data on incoming shipments to identify suspicious shipments for examination. According to port officials, local targeting methods include developing local user-defined rules, generating cargo hold requests, and conducting port-based operations, which are targeting exercises conducted within a specific time frame on specific shipments of products at specific ports.[22] Port officials also told us that the amount of local targeting conducted varies based on how individual officials prioritize their responsibilities to manage their workloads.

Phase 3: Examining Products

Based on the results of the various targeting methods, port officials may examine products in the identified shipments to determine whether the products are covered by exclusion orders. Officials at the ports we visited told us that they will frequently seek guidance from IPR Branch officials when determining whether a product is covered by an exclusion order. At the initiative of the complainant, CBP officials may receive training in determining how products in shipments may infringe upon the intellectual property rights of the complainant's product. For example, Electronics Center officials said that a company that produces inkjet printer cartridges contacted CBP and arranged to provide training to port officials on the features of its cartridges and how to determine if imported products violate the company's patents. In addition, CBP officials may use specialized equipment to gain additional information on the imported products. For example, to quickly determine if imported pills contain formulas that are covered by an exclusion order, port officials told us they use handheld tools that can scan powder in pills and report the formula used. CBP officials can also consult a network of six internal labs to conduct analyses on products as part of their fact finding. For example, Electronics Center officials said they use the electronics lab in San Francisco, California, if they must examine a high-tech product with complex patents, such as mobile phone software or hardware.

Phase 4: Excluding Infringing Shipments

If port officials determine that a product is covered by an exclusion order, CBP excludes the shipment from entering U.S. commerce and notifies the importer of its action. At this point, the importer may decide to return the shipment to the port of origin or export it to another country.[23] After an importer's first excluded shipment, ITC generally will issue a seizure and forfeiture order to CBP, which directs CBP to seize, rather than merely deny entry to, any future shipments of the same infringing products from the importer.[24] Once ITC issues the seizure and forfeiture order, CBP officials said they update the trade alert and targeting instructions in the targeting system so that port officials know to seize any future shipments of the infringing products.[25] However, if port officials determine that a product is not covered by an exclusion order, the shipment is released for entry into the United States.[26]

Port officials enter data on excluded or seized shipments into CBP's exclusion order notification and tracking system. Developed in 2010 in response to a GAO recommendation, the system enables port officials to enter excluded shipments into the system and document the date, time, location, and action taken for each excluded shipment.[27] The system then electronically notifies the port director and the IPR Branch of the exclusion or seizure. The port director sends a letter explaining the exclusion or seizure to the importer, the IPR Branch, and the ITC.

When CBP seizes counterfeit products at ports, it notifies the affected intellectual property rights holders. However, when CBP denies entry to or seizes products that are covered by an exclusion order, CBP does not inform the complainants. In our 2008 report, we found that some companies do not consider CBP's enforcement of exclusion orders to be transparent because of this lack of communication from CBP, which may impede the complainant's ability to protect its intellectual property rights, independently and in collaboration with CBP. We recommended in that report that CBP examine whether it has the statutory authority needed to develop regulations that would allow CBP to notify complainants of infringing shipments that have been excluded, and if authorized, to develop such regulations. [28] CBP subsequently determined that it did not have the required statutory authority and identified the need for legislative action, which it believed would help strengthen enforcement efforts. According to CBP officials, increased communication with complainants regarding exclusions could provide complainants with the opportunity to provide CBP with information to help revise its targeting strategies. In March 2011, the administration recommended that Congress give DHS the authority to notify intellectual property rights holders when infringing products have been excluded or seized pursuant to an exclusion order.[29] According to CBP, as of September 2014, Congress had not enacted this recommendation into law.

CBP's enforcement of exclusion orders from fiscal years 2010 through 2014 resulted in the exclusion or seizure of 158 shipments of various kinds of products. See table 1.

CBP officials explained that several factors may limit the number of shipments that CBP excludes:

- First, unlike the importers of counterfeit products, the respondents in exclusion order cases tend to be legitimate companies that seek to be in compliance with trade laws; thus, they generally do not intentionally attempt to import infringing products.

- Second, respondents may work to resolve issues, such as finding new suppliers, obtaining licenses, or redesigning products, so that they do not have shipments of products excluded at the ports.
- Third, the conditions related to the underlying patent, trademark, or other protectable rights associated with the exclusion order may change, such that the complainant or respondent or both are no longer in business, or the infringing products are no longer made.

Table 1. Number of Shipments and Examples of Products Excluded or Seized as a Result of U.S. Customs and Border Protection's Enforcement of Exclusion Orders, Fiscal Year 2010 through Fiscal Year 2014

Fiscal year[a]	Number of shipments excluded or seized	Examples of products in excluded shipments
2010	4	Magic cube puzzles, ink cartridges, coaxial cable connectors
2011	22	Plastic plates and plastic lids, ink cartridges, cigarettes, coaxial cable connectors, transceivers, energy drinks
2012	64	Plastic food storage containers with resealable lids, ink cartridges, footwear, sucralose, cigarettes, coaxial cable connectors, phones, toner cartridges
2013	34	Ink sticks, ink cartridges, footwear, cigarettes, cell phone cases
2014	34	Laminate flooring, footwear, digital multimeters, cigarettes, cell phone cases, massagers
Total	158	

Source: GAO analysis of U.S. Customs and Border Protection (CBP) data. | GAO-15-78.

[a] For fiscal year 2010, the data are incomplete. U.S. Customs and Border Protection (CBP) did not begin tracking exclusions in its exclusion order notification and tracking system until September 16, 2010. For fiscal year 2014, CBP provided data on exclusions through April 30, 2014.

- Finally, CBP officials noted that data on excluded shipments are underreported because of alternative actions that can be taken by CBP for shipments of products that are covered by an exclusion order but are also protected by a recorded trademark. In such cases, CBP officials will seize the shipment as a trademark violation rather than deny it entry under an exclusion order. Officials told us that complainants would rather have CBP seize these infringing products than risk the possibility that importers might try to reship the products to the United States through another port.

CBP Uses an Administrative Ruling Process in Advance of Importing to Determine Whether Products Are Covered by Exclusion Orders

Prior to importing, a company may request that CBP determine through its administrative ruling process whether its products fall within the scope of an exclusion order.[30] According to CBP officials, companies may redesign their products in an attempt to remove products from the scope of exclusion orders. In other instances, companies may request an administrative ruling before they start to import (1) a redesigned product, (2) a new product, or (3) a product that was not accused at ITC but is potentially within the scope of the exclusion order. Upon a company's request and when CBP determines it to be in the interest of the sound administration of customs and related laws, CBP will undertake to issue a ruling letter on whether the product in question is subject to exclusion. Figure 4 provides an overview of the administrative ruling process CBP uses to determine whether a new or redesigned product is covered by an exclusion order.

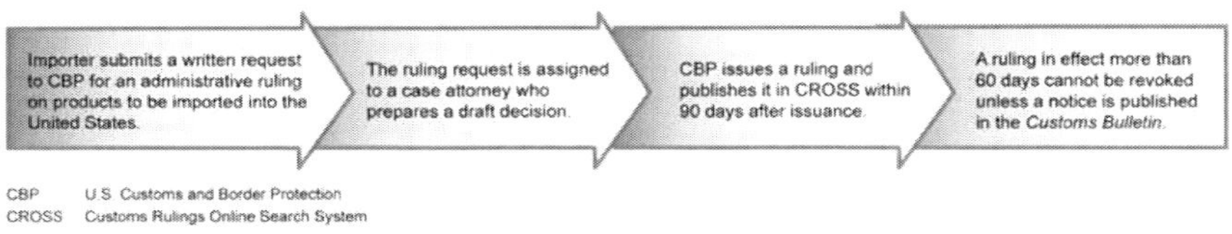

Source: GAO analysis of CBP documents and interviews woth CBP officials.| GAO-15-78.

Figure 4. U.S. Customs and Border Protection Process for Administrative Rulings to Determine Prior to Importation Whether a Product Falls within the Scope of an Exclusion Order.

Requests for an administrative ruling are submitted in writing to CBP's IPR Branch. Each request is entered in CBP's Regulations and Rulings Directorate's case management system. Upon receipt, a ruling request is assigned to a case attorney who reviews the request and other relevant materials, including the exclusion order, a sample of the product, the patent and the prosecution history, and the ITC's initial and final determinations. If the case attorney has a question about a specific point in the ITC record, the attorney may contact ITC to seek clarification on the specific issue.[31] At this time, CBP also meets with the respondent to discuss the request for an administrative ruling.

A CBP administrative ruling is generally effective upon its issuance by CBP. Within 90 days from issuance, the decision is made public and published in CBP's Customs Ruling Online Search System. [32] Once the ruling is public, copies of the decision will be provided to the complainant and the ITC. For rulings that have been in effect for less than 60 days, generally, CBP may decide to revoke a ruling simply by giving written notice to the person to whom the original was issued.[33] A revocation may occur, for example, if CBP discovers that facts relevant to the ruling were misrepresented in the request, or if changing circumstances materially affect the basis of CBP's determination in the ruling. After 60 days, CBP must adhere to additional requirements if it decides to revoke a ruling, such as publishing a notice proposing the revocation and inviting public comment.[34] CBP officials noted that if CBP issues an administrative ruling that approves the new or redesigned product for entry, the product is still potentially subject to examination at the ports to ensure compliance. From September 16, 2010, through April 30, 2014, the IPR Branch issued 18 rulings, of which 13 ruled that the products were not infringing and could enter U.S. commerce. In addition, the importer with an administrative ruling that approves a redesigned product may also ask for a CBP certification on its product. The CBP certification confirms that the redesigned product is not covered by an exclusion order.[35]

Currently, CBP's administrative ruling process is an *ex parte* process where only the importer requesting the ruling participates in the process, not the complainants in the original case that resulted in the exclusion order. IPR Branch officials told us that they are developing a proposal for an *inter partes* process within CBP's administrative ruling process that would enable the complainant as well as the importer that has requested a ruling to provide information before CBP issues its administrative ruling on the product. The proposed process would allow both the complainant and the importer to make arguments and rebut those of the other party. IPR Branch officials noted that the proposed *inter partes* process will have advantages over the current process because it will gather information from both the complainant and the importer, potentially enabling CBP to expedite its administrative ruling process. IPR Branch officials could provide no estimate as to when the proposed *inter partes* process will be finalized.[36]

In anticipation of a possible request for an administrative ruling and to increase their understanding of the exclusion order in general, CBP officials may meet with officials from the ITC and with the complainants and respondents involved in the ITC's Section 337 investigations. Officials said that these meetings can provide them with useful information, especially if an administrative ruling is being considered or requested by the respondent. For example, since the summer of 2013, according to IPR Branch officials, CBP and ITC have regularly held meetings upon the issuance of a new exclusion order. CBP and ITC officials characterized the nature of these meetings as limited to CBP seeking clarification on issues that ITC addressed during its investigation. IPR Branch officials also access a secure web-based repository established by ITC to review the ITC's administrative record, such as the initial and final determinations and documentation of the ITC proceedings, to understand the questions of law and issues of fact raised in the investigation. In addition to their meetings with ITC, CBP officials from the IPR Branch and the Electronics Center may meet separately with complainants and respondents on an informal basis during the Section 337 investigation or after an exclusion order is issued. These meetings are typically initiated by the complainants and respondents, although the Electronics Center is in regular communication with companies it serves as part of its mission. During these meetings, the complainants may share useful information on the intellectual property rights at issue and highlight relevant findings in the investigation, while respondents may explore CBP's management of its exclusion order enforcement process at the ports contains weaknesses that result in inefficiencies and an increased risk of infringing products entering U.S. commerce. First, CBP does not routinely review ITC's list of exclusion orders or take other action to ensure that a trade alert has been posted to its intranet for each order. As a result of our audit, CBP reviewed ITC's list of exclusion orders as of April 30, 2014, and reported that it had posted trade alerts for 83 of the 94 exclusion orders; however, it posted 17 of the 83 trade alerts after our request for data. Without routinely taking action to ensure that trade alerts are posted to the intranet, there is an increased risk that infringing products could enter into U.S. commerce. Second, CBP does not routinely review ITC's list of exclusion orders to identify orders that may be candidates for rescission by ITC.[37] As a result of our inquiry, CBP identified 6 exclusion orders as possible candidates for ITC rescission. Requesting rescission of exclusion orders could enable CBP to focus its enforcement efforts more effectively and efficiently. Third, CBP's products are covered by an exclusion order or discuss potential redesigns for their infringing products. Electronics Center officials said they met with 16 complainants and 31 respondents in fiscal year 2013 to discuss information on supply chains, transportation modes, ports of entry, and distribution networks. In addition, since fiscal year 2013, the Electronics Center has collaborated with the IPR Branch on five administrative rulings.

MANAGEMENT WEAKNESSES IN CBP'S ENFORCEMENT PROCESS AT PORTS RESULT IN INEFFICIENCIES AND INCREASED RISK OF INFRINGING PRODUCTS ENTERING U.S. COMMERCE

CBP's management of its exclusion order enforcement process at the ports contains weaknesses that result in inefficiencies and an increased risk of infringing products entering U.S. commerce. First, CBP does not routinely review ITC's list of exclusion orders or take other action to ensure that a trade alert has been posted to its intranet for each order. As a result of our audit, CBP reviewed ITC's list of exclusion orders as of April 30, 2014, and reported that it had posted trade alerts for 83 of the 94 exclusion orders; however, it posted 17 of the 83 trade alerts after our request for data. Without routinely taking action to ensure that trade alerts are posted to the intranet, there is an increased risk that infringing products could enter into U.S. commerce. Second, CBP does not routinely review ITC's list of exclusion orders to identify orders that may be candidates for rescission by ITC.37 As a result of our inquiry, CBP identified 6 exclusion orders as possible candidates for ITC rescission. Requesting rescission of exclusion orders could enable CBP to focus its enforcement efforts more effectively and efficiently. Third, CBP's guidance lacks time frames for issuing trade alerts, which prevents CBP from monitoring timeliness. We found that it took CBP from 2 days to 3 months to request a posting of a trade alert to the intranet during the period from October 2009 through April 2014. Without actively managing trade alerts and establishing time frames for posting alerts, CBP management cannot hold staff accountable for timely enforcement of exclusion orders, and there is an increased risk of infringing products entering U.S. commerce. We reported on similar weaknesses in our 2008 report on federal intellectual property enforcement efforts at the border.[38]

CBP Provides Exclusion Order Guidance within Several Documents

CBP's IPR Branch has issued official guidance on enforcing exclusion orders and tracking exclusion order enforcement. This guidance is found in a federal regulation,[39] an internal directive, and an internal document detailing standard operating procedures. IPR Branch officials said that the standard operating procedures issued in 2010 provide the most current guidance on exclusion order enforcement.

CBP Does Not Routinely Review ITC Exclusion Orders or Take Other Action to Ensure Enforcement Coverage and Efficiency

CBP does not routinely review ITC exclusion orders or take other action to ensure that trade alerts exist or to identify orders that may be candidates for rescission by ITC. As previously discussed, the first phase of the process for enforcing exclusion orders at the ports involves issuing trade alerts to trigger CBP's targeting and enforcement efforts. CBP guidance on exclusion order enforcement states that the IPR Branch will issue trade alerts with enforcement instructions to national targeting groups and local port officials; the IPR Branch issues trade alerts by posting them to the CBP intranet.[40]

While federal internal control standards state that management should conduct periodic reviews, reconciliations, or comparisons of data to assess the quality of performance over time, CBP's guidance does not require IPR Branch officials to conduct routine reviews of exclusion orders for these purposes.[41]

IPR Branch officials told us that they had not conducted a review of ITC's list of exclusion orders in 5 years. In response to our request for data, IPR Branch officials reviewed ITC exclusion orders in effect as of April 30, 2014, to determine whether the IPR Branch had issued a trade alert for each order. According to ITC data, there were 94 exclusion orders that CBP was required to enforce as of that date. The IPR Branch reported that it had posted trade alerts on CBP's intranet for 83 of the 94 exclusion orders. However, our analysis of the data found that the IPR Branch had posted trade alerts on the intranet for 17 of these orders in early April 2014, after receiving our data request.[42]

For the remaining 11 of the 94 exclusion orders, IPR Branch officials reported that they had not posted trade alerts to the intranet, as stated in CBP guidance. These 11 exclusion orders, plus the 17 exclusion orders posted on the intranet in April 2014, were part of a group of 28 older exclusion orders, for which IPR Branch officials explained that they had created trade alerts either in paper form or in another electronic system. However, they had never transferred these alerts to the intranet when CBP began issuing trade alerts on its intranet in 2004. As a result of our review, officials found they had not created a trade alert in any form for 1 of these 28 exclusion orders. Figure 5 shows the status of CBP's trade alerts for exclusion orders as of April 30, 2014.

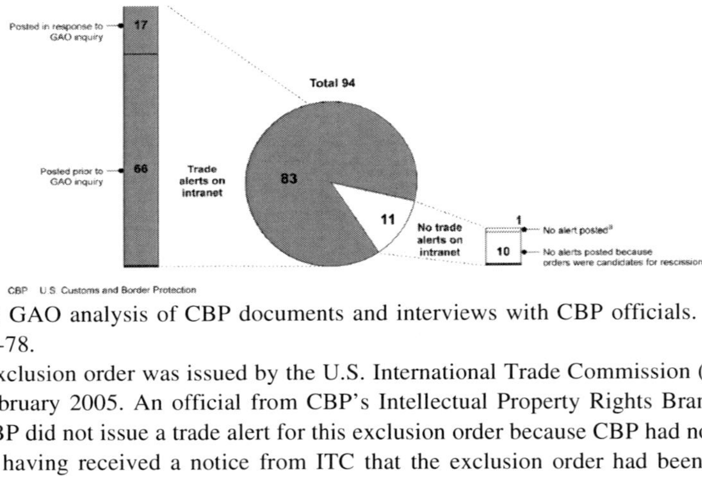

CBP U.S. Customs and Border Protection

Source: GAO analysis of CBP documents and interviews with CBP officials. | GAO-15-78.

[a]This exclusion order was issued by the U.S. International Trade Commission (ITC) in February 2005. An official from CBP's Intellectual Property Rights Branch said CBP did not issue a trade alert for this exclusion order because CBP had no record of having received a notice from ITC that the exclusion order had been issued. ITC officials provided us with a copy of an ITC letter notifying CBP of the exclusion order; however, these officials did not have documentation confirming CBP's receipt of the letter. According to ITC officials, in 2005 CBP officials would receive hand-delivered copies of the exclusion order; however, ITC officials now transmit exclusion orders via e-mail. As a result of our review, CBP officials said they contacted the complainant involved in the exclusion order in July 2014 and were informed that the complainant was unaware of any infringing importations following the exclusion order's issuance in February 2005. CBP issued a trade alert for this exclusion order in July 2014.

Figure 5. Status of U.S. Customs and Border Protection's Trade Alerts for Exclusion Orders as of April 30, 2014.

For 10 of the 11 exclusion orders that did not have trade alerts on the intranet, IPR Branch officials said they decided not to post trade alerts to the CBP intranet in April 2014 because officials considered these orders candidates for ITC rescission. According to a federal regulation, any person may file a petition to request that ITC rescind an exclusion order if he or she believes that changes in conditions of fact or law or the public interest require rescission.[43] According to an IPR Branch official, CBP believed that the conditions related to the underlying patent, trademark, or other protectable rights for these 10 orders had changed; for example, the complainant named in one exclusion order was no longer in business. IPR Branch officials later decided that they would not request that ITC rescind 2 of these orders because discussions with complainants established that the exclusion orders should remain active; the IPR Branch posted trade alerts for these to the intranet in July 2014. In addition, according to IPR Branch officials, the intellectual property rights protected by 2 other exclusion orders that were candidates for rescission expired in July 2014. As a result, the IPR Branch sent a letter to ITC in August 2014 requesting that it rescind 6 exclusion orders.[44]

CBP's lack of routine reviews of exclusion orders has resulted in gaps and inefficiencies in CBP's exclusion order enforcement. For the 27 exclusion orders with trade alerts in either paper form or in another electronic system, IPR-NTAG reported that it had not implemented national targeting strategies for these exclusion orders. If any targeting occurred, IPR Branch officials said it would have been initiated at the port level.[45] As a result of these targeting gaps, there is an increased risk that infringing products could have entered into U.S. commerce.[46] For the 1 exclusion order without a trade alert, a routine review of ITC's exclusion orders by CBP officials would have identified the error sooner. In addition, with routine reviews of ITC's list of exclusion orders, officials could have identified the ones that were candidates for rescission sooner and requested that ITC rescind them, potentially allowing CBP to more effectively and efficiently focus its enforcement efforts. This is not a new problem. In our 2008 report, we found similar weaknesses.[47] We reported that CBP had posted trade alerts to its intranet for 24 of the 66 orders that were in effect as of July 2007, and had not yet transferred paper alerts for 15 older exclusion orders to the intranet because of limited resources. We also noted that CBP had trade alerts for 5 orders that had expired or had been rescinded.

CBP Lacks Established Time Frames for Issuing Trade Alerts

IPR Branch officials have not established a time frame in CBP's guidance for issuing trade alerts, which prevents officials from monitoring timeliness. Federal internal control standards state that management should establish procedures, such as time frames, to ensure that the agency is meeting its objectives and document these procedures in policies or directives. In addition, monitoring the effectiveness of internal control activities, such as determining timeliness, should occur in the normal course of business.[48]

An IPR Branch official said that the IPR Branch's approach to issuing trade alerts has evolved since 2006 toward an increased emphasis on timeliness. IPR Branch officials said they generally try to post a trade alert to the CBP intranet within 5 workdays of receiving an exclusion order from ITC. Prior to 2006, the official told us that the IPR Branch wanted to gain a full understanding of the exclusion order and the intellectual property rights in question before issuing a trade alert, but more recently, according to this official, the IPR Branch has placed more importance on providing information as quickly as possible so the national targeting groups can more promptly develop targeting methods.

Our analysis of CBP's data shows that for 33 exclusion orders issued from October 1, 2009, through April 30, 2014, the IPR Branch generally took anywhere from 2 days to about 3 months to request a posting of a trade alert to the intranet.[49] For 9 of the 33 exclusion orders, about 27 percent, CBP requested a posting of trade alerts to the CBP intranet within 5 workdays of exclusion order issuance. Without established time frames for issuing trade alerts in its guidance on enforcing exclusion orders, CBP cannot do the following:

- CBP cannot monitor and assess its performance on timeliness, which increases the risk of enforcement gaps. The longer it takes the national targeting groups to receive trade alerts and develop targeting approaches that will identify shipments for examination at the ports, the greater the risk that infringing products covered by an exclusion order may be permitted entry into U.S. commerce.
- CBP management cannot hold staff accountable for timely enforcement. Effective internal control, such as establishing time frames for performance, is a key factor in achieving agency missions and program results through improved accountability.[50]

CBP uses two processes to enforce exclusion orders: one that identifies shipments with infringing products arriving at the ports and one that determines in advance of importing whether products are covered by exclusion orders. These processes leverage information from both the complainants and respondents involved in Section 337 cases adjudicated by the ITC that result in exclusion orders. CBP's management of its process for enforcing exclusion orders at the ports has weaknesses that result in inefficiencies and enforcement gaps. First, CBP does not routinely review exclusion orders to ensure that trade alerts exist for all ITC exclusion orders. We found that for about one-fourth of the exclusion orders in effect during our review, CBP had not posted trade alerts on its intranet until after our data request. Without an alert, it would be difficult for CBP components to enforce an exclusion order. Second, CBP lacks an established procedure that would enable it to routinely determine those exclusion orders that are candidates for ITC rescission, potentially resulting in fewer exclusion orders and trade alerts to manage, which would allow CBP to better focus its enforcement efforts. Third, CBP has not established a time frame for trade alert issuance in CBP's guidance, which prevents management from monitoring timeliness in issuing trade alerts. In our 2008 report examining CBP's intellectual property enforcement, we found similar weaknesses in its management of exclusion order enforcement. Lacking guidance on time frames for key steps in exclusion order enforcement, CBP officials cannot hold staff accountable for timely enforcement, which is critical to reducing the risk of infringing products entering U.S. commerce.

Recommendations for Executive Action

To improve CBP's management of its process for enforcing exclusion orders, we recommend that the Secretary of Homeland Security direct the CBP Commissioner to take the following three actions to update CBP's internal guidance with requirements to

- Routinely ensure that trade alerts are posted on the CBP intranet for each exclusion order.
- Routinely identify any orders whose changed conditions merit a CBP request that ITC rescind them.
- Monitor timeliness by establishing time frames for issuing trade alerts for exclusion orders and reviewing performance against these standards.

AGENCY COMMENTS AND OUR EVALUATION

We provided a draft of this report to CBP, ITC, and USTR for their review and comment. We received technical comments from CBP, ITC, and USTR, which we incorporated where appropriate.

In its written comments, CBP concurred with two of our three recommendations: to update CBP's internal guidance with requirements to routinely ensure that trade alerts are posted on the CBP intranet for each exclusion order and monitor timeliness by establishing time frames for issuing trade alerts for exclusion orders and reviewing performance against these standards. As part of its efforts to implement these two recommendations, CBP reported that it is developing a template for case attorneys to use in developing future trade alerts and that it is updating its internal standard operating procedures with requirements for CBP staff to monitor the timeliness of posting trade alerts on the CBP intranet. While these are positive actions, it is not yet clear whether they will address the recommendations to the full extent. We will continue to monitor CBP's actions in this area.

CBP did not concur with our recommendation to update its guidance with a requirement to routinely identify any orders whose changed conditions merit a CBP request that ITC rescind them. CBP noted that there is no statutory or regulatory authority mandating that it monitor the ITC's list of exclusion orders to determine if changed conditions of law or fact would warrant the rescission of any of the orders. In addition, CBP asserted that ITC, as the issuing agency of exclusion orders, and the relevant complainants, or both have responsibility for ensuring that the list of outstanding exclusion orders is current. As we state in the report, any person may file a petition to request that ITC rescind an exclusion order if he or she believes that changes in conditions of fact or law or the public interest require rescission. While CBP is not specifically mandated to conduct a routine review of exclusion orders to identify candidates for ITC rescission, CBP is the enforcement agency of exclusion orders. Based on internal control standards, we reiterate that it is good management practice for CBP to conduct these reviews that could potentially allow it to more effectively and efficiently focus its efforts by reducing the number of exclusion orders it is responsible for enforcing. For example, in response to our audit, CBP conducted such a review, identified six exclusion orders that it believed were candidates for ITC rescission, and submitted a letter requesting that ITC rescind the orders. Thus, we continue to believe that our recommendation is valid and that CBP should fully implement it.

CBP also noted in its written response that the report would have been more value-added if it had included additional discussion on the challenges of making patent infringement determinations at the border under the time constraints imposed by statute, or on the development of the *inter partes* process. These issues CBP mentions were outside the scope of our review. However, our report does discuss CBP's current *ex parte* administrative ruling process and provided details on CBP's development of an *inter partes* process that would enable both the complainant and the importer to provide information during the administrative ruling process. As of October 2014, CBP officials could not provide an estimate as to when the *inter partes* process would be finalized.

Kimberly M. Gianopoulos
Director
International Affairs and Trade

APPENDIX I: OBJECTIVES, SCOPE, AND METHODOLOGY

This report reviews the efforts of U.S. Customs and Border Protection (CBP) to enforce exclusion orders issued by the U.S. International Trade Commission (ITC). Specifically, we (1) examine CBP's processes for enforcing exclusion orders and (2) assess CBP's management of its enforcement process at ports of entry. In this report, we neither take a position on, nor do we address, the matters pending in ongoing litigation between Microsoft and the U.S. Department of Homeland Security related to CBP's enforcement of an exclusion order.[1]

To provide an overview of ITC exclusion orders, we first reviewed the list of exclusion orders on the ITC website as of April 30, 2014, to determine the number of exclusion orders that CBP was responsible for enforcing. Though ITC's list named 96 exclusion orders, we interviewed agency officials to assess the reliability of the data, and ITC provided clarification on duplicate orders or consolidated investigations. As a result of our interviews, ITC confirmed that 94 exclusion orders were in effect as of April 30, 2014. We also interviewed ITC officials regarding the underlying data systems and the checks, controls, and reviews used to generate the data and ensure their accuracy and reliability. We found the data sufficiently reliable for the purpose of this report. We then analyzed CBP data on these exclusion orders to determine characteristics such as the type of exclusion order (general or limited); the protected intellectual property rights (e.g., trademark, copyright, patent); and the Harmonized Tariff Schedule categorization numbers for the products covered by the exclusion orders. We analyzed these numbers to determine the types of commodities protected by exclusion orders. To assess the reliability of CBP's data, we interviewed agency officials regarding the underlying data systems and the checks, controls, and reviews used to generate the data and ensure their accuracy and reliability. We found the data sufficiently reliable for the purpose of this report.

To examine CBP's process for enforcing exclusion orders at ports of entry, we reviewed CBP's internal guidance related to exclusion order enforcement. We interviewed agency officials at CBP, ITC, the Office of Management and Budget's Office of the Intellectual Property Enforcement Coordinator, and the Office of the United States Trade Representative in Washington, D.C., to discuss each agency's role in facilitating or informing CBP's enforcement of exclusion orders. We interviewed CBP headquarters officials to understand CBP's process for issuing trade alerts and communicating them to national targeting groups and local port officials. Using the list of exclusion orders on ITC's website as of April 30, 2014, we analyzed CBP data to determine whether CBP had issued a trade alert for each exclusion order. To assess the reliability of CBP's data, we reviewed issued trade alerts for each of the exclusion orders and interviewed agency officials regarding the checks, controls, and reviews used to generate the data and ensure their accuracy and reliability. We found the data sufficiently reliable for the purpose of this report.

To determine how CBP develops targeting strategies for enforcing exclusion orders, we interviewed agency officials from CBP's national targeting groups for exclusion order enforcement: the Intellectual Property Rights National Targeting and Analysis Group in Long Beach and the Electronics Center of Excellence and Expertise in Los Angeles. To understand how CBP examines products and excludes infringing shipments at the ports, we interviewed agency officials at four ports: Buffalo, New York; John F. Kennedy International Airport in Jamaica, New York; Los Angeles/Long Beach Seaport in Long Beach, California; and Los Angeles International Airport in Los Angeles, California. We selected ports with experience in enforcing exclusion orders based on CBP exclusions data from September 16, 2010, through April 30, 2014;[2] during this period, a total of 12 ports excluded shipments as part of CBP's enforcement of exclusion orders. We also selected ports where we could discuss and observe CBP's exclusion order enforcement process when processing shipments arriving by land, sea, and air. One selected port, Buffalo, processes shipments arriving by land; two ports, John F. Kennedy International Airport and Los Angeles International Airport, process shipments arriving by air; and one port, Los Angeles/Long Beach Seaport, processes shipments arriving by sea. We interviewed port officials to obtain information on training received and equipment used by CBP officials to determine whether products in shipments are covered by exclusion orders. In addition to interviewing port officials, we observed them as they targeted and examined shipments, and seized shipments as required. The information gathered from our site visits cannot be generalized to all ports and field offices.

To understand CBP's future exclusion order enforcement efforts, we interviewed CBP officials from the Industrial and Manufacturing Materials Center of Excellence and Expertise in Buffalo, New York, and the Pharmaceuticals, Health, and Chemicals Center of Excellence and Expertise in New York, New York. Officials from these centers provided us with an overview of how they will eventually take responsibility for enforcing exclusion orders related to the industry sectors that their centers cover.

We analyzed CBP data on the number of shipments excluded from entry from September 16, 2010, through April 30, 2014, including the number of exclusions by fiscal year and the types of products excluded during this period. CBP officials noted that data on excluded shipments are underreported because of alternative actions that can be taken by CBP for shipments of products that are covered by an exclusion order but are also protected by a recorded trademark. In such cases, CBP officials said they will seize the shipment as a trademark violation rather than exclude it under an exclusion order. To assess the reliability of CBP's data, we interviewed agency officials regarding the underlying data systems and the checks, controls, and reviews used to generate the data and ensure their accuracy and reliability. We found the data sufficiently reliable for the purpose of this report.

To assess how CBP manages its exclusion order enforcement process, we evaluated CBP's management of the process against CBP criteria in its exclusion order guidance, found in a CBP regulation,[3] an internal directive, and a document outlining standard operating procedures. We also evaluated CBP's management of the process against requirements established in federal internal control standards, such as establishing procedures to ensure that the agency is meeting its objectives, documenting these procedures in policies or directives, and monitoring the effectiveness of internal control activities in the normal course of business.[4] We interviewed CBP officials from the Intellectual Property Rights Branch in the Regulations and Rulings Directorate to discuss how they manage the issuance of trade alerts. We reviewed CBP's written guidance on exclusion order enforcement to determine whether CBP documents time frames for issuing trade alerts. Using ITC exclusion order issuance dates and CBP's data on trade alert issuance dates, we analyzed the number of workdays that CBP officials took to request posting of trade alerts to the CBP intranet for exclusion orders issued from October 1, 2009, through April 30, 2014. To assess the reliability of CBP data, we interviewed agency officials and reviewed underlying data sources. CBP trade alert data are for the dates on which CBP officials requested a posting of trade alerts to the CBP intranet and not the dates on which the alerts were actually posted. We found the data sufficiently reliable for the purpose of this report.

To describe CBP's process for determining, in advance of importing certain products, whether those products are covered by exclusion orders, we reviewed regulations outlining CBP's administrative ruling process. [5] We also interviewed CBP officials from the Intellectual Property Rights Branch in the Regulations and Rulings Directorate to discuss how the ruling process works and CBP's proposed changes to the process. We interviewed ITC officials to discuss the extent to which ITC informs this process by providing information on the exclusion orders and the administrative records associated with ITC investigations.

We conducted this performance audit from November 2013 to November 2014 in accordance with generally accepted government auditing standards. Those standards require that we plan and perform the audit to obtain sufficient, appropriate evidence to provide a reasonable basis for our findings and conclusions based on our audit objectives. We believe that the evidence obtained provides a reasonable basis for our findings and conclusions based on our audit objectives.

APPENDIX II: U.S. CUSTOMS AND BORDER PROTECTION OFFICES RESPONSIBLE FOR EXCLUSION ORDER ENFORCEMENT

U.S. Customs and Border Protection's (CBP) Office of International Trade and Office of Field Operations are responsible for coordinating CBP's efforts to enforce exclusion orders. Several units under these two offices have key responsibilities in CBP's enforcement process and its related administrative ruling process (see fig. 6).

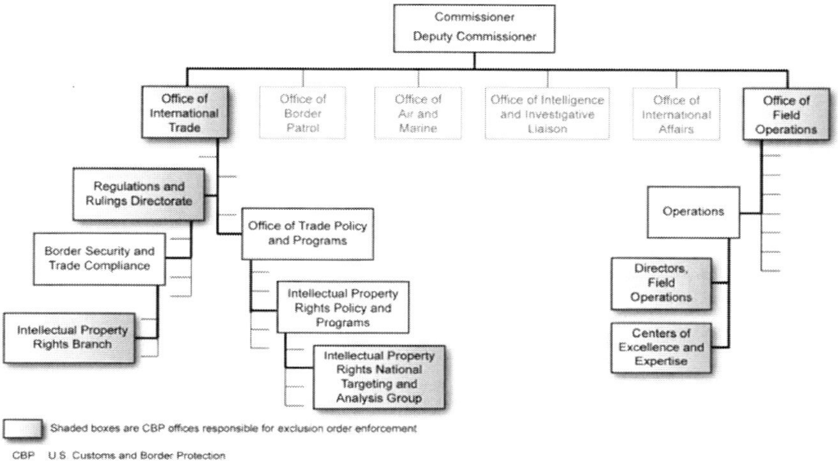

Source: GAO analysis of CBP documents. | GAO-15-78.

Figure 6. Key Customs and Border Protection Offices Involved in Exclusion Order Enforcement.

APPENDIX III: U.S. CUSTOMS AND BORDER PROTECTION CENTERS OF EXCELLENCE AND EXPERTISE

In 2012, U.S. Customs and Border Protection (CBP) established 10 Centers of Excellence and Expertise to provide trade information and processing for the trade community and U.S. government partners. While in their early stages, the centers are intended to facilitate legitimate trade, increase CBP's industry-based knowledge, and assist CBP in addressing risks and protecting intellectual property rights more efficiently and effectively. Each center is specific to a single industry sector (see table 2).

The centers, with staff located at ports of entry throughout the United States, operate as virtual organizations that centralize industry sector expertise. For example, the Electronics Center of Excellence and Expertise is located in Los Angeles but has staff located in other ports that deal with imports of electronics, such as El Paso, Texas; Memphis, Tennessee; Cleveland, Ohio; and San Diego, California. Of the 10 centers, this is the one with a role in the enforcement of exclusion orders as of November 2014 (see sidebar).

Table 2. U.S. Customs and Border Protection Centers of Excellence and Expertise Centers

Centers	Location
Agriculture and Prepared Products	Miami
Apparel, Footwear, and Textiles	San Francisco
Automotive and Aerospace	Detroit
Base Metals	Chicago
Consumer Products and Mass Merchandising	Atlanta
Electronics	Los Angeles
Industrial and Manufacturing Materials	Buffalo
Machinery	Laredo
Petroleum, Natural Gas, and Minerals	Houston
Pharmaceuticals, Health, and Chemicals	New York

All centers employ trade specialists with a range of account management and operational skills, including import, supply chain, and operations specialists. Importers can go directly to their assigned center for assistance, instead of consulting CBP officials at multiple ports of entry. Center officials are expected to continuously update their industry-related expertise for exclusion orders by attending and participating in industry conferences, trade forums, enforcement seminars, and online training.

Electronics Center of Excellence and Expertise, Los Angeles, California

The Electronics Center of Excellence and Expertise (Electronics Center) is the most developed of the U.S. Customs and Border Protection's (CBP) 10 industry-specialized virtual centers. As of November 2014, it was the only center with a role in enforcing exclusion orders, specifically the enforcement of electronics-related exclusion orders. In fiscal year 2013, the Electronics Center conducted targeting for 32 exclusion orders.

Electronics Center staff members meet informally with the complainants and respondents involved in an investigation before the U.S. International Trade Commission (ITC) issues an exclusion order. CBP intends for this model of advanced collaboration to speed up the exclusion order enforcement process because staff will better understand the products involved and the complainant and respondent companies' trading patterns.

In addition, the center's specialists assist CBP's Intellectual Property Rights (IPR) Branch in developing trade alertsfor exclusion orders involving electronic technologies and products.

The IPR Branch has collaborated with the Electronics Center in proactively working with companies to avertthe importation of infringing products at ports and to place CBP in a better position to rule on admissibility, rulings, and certification. The Electronics Center also conducts its own targeting of shipments for exclusion order enforcement, with assistance, if necessary, from CBP's Intellectual Property Rights National Targeting and Analysis Group.

Source: U.S. Customs and Border Protection. | GAO-15-78.

End Notes

[1] Department of Commerce, Intellectual Property and the U.S. Economy: Industries in Focus (Washington, D.C.: March 2012).

[2] 19 U.S.C. § 1337.

[3] ITC can issue a "cease and desist" order directing the violating parties to cease certain actions in addition to or in lieu of an exclusion order. 19 U.S.C. § 1337.

[4] See Administrative Rulings, 19 C.F.R. Part 177. These regulations detail CBP's general processes to respond to an importer's request to obtain certainty in its import transaction about the admissibility of its product.

[5] The litigation involves CBP's enforcement efforts pertaining to an exclusion order issued by ITC, finding a violation of Section 337 because certain Motorola products had infringed Microsoft's patent rights. Microsoft Corporation v. Dep't of Homeland Sec. et al, 1:13-cv 01063-RWR (D.D.C. July 12, 2013).

[6] We used data starting on September 16, 2010, because CBP started tracking exclusions in its exclusion order notification and tracking system on this date.

[7] Office of Management and Budget, Management's Responsibility for Internal Control, OMB Circular No. A-123 (Washington, D.C.: Dec. 21, 2004) and GAO, Standards for Internal Control in the Federal Government, GAO/AIMD-00-21.3.1 (Washington, D.C.: November 1999)

[8] 19 U.S.C. § 1337 (d)(1). The ITC may also issue a temporary exclusion order if the requirements of Section 337(e) are met (19 U.S.C. § 1337(e)) or where the named respondents are found in default under Section 337(g) (19 U.S.C. § 1337(g)).

[9] 19 U.S.C. § 1337(a).

[10] Generally outlined in 19 C.F.R. Part 210 and 19 U.S.C. § 1337.

[11] The ITC will decide whether to institute an investigation within 30 days unless certain conditions apply such as exceptional circumstances that preclude adherence to the 30- day deadline. Moreover, the ITC will determine whether to institute an investigation within 35 days if a motion for temporary relief is filed with the complaint. 19 C.F.R. § 210.10(a).

[12] Public interest includes consideration of public health and welfare, competitive conditions in the U.S. economy, the production of like or directly competitive articles, and the interests of U.S. consumers.

[13] Upon the ITC's issuance of an exclusion order, the USTR, on behalf of the President, begins a 60-day review process to decide whether to disapprove the ITC's determination for policy reasons. During this review period, companies are allowed to continue importing if they secure a bond, assuming a bond is required. Usually the USTR takes no action with respect to the ITC's determination and the exclusion order remains in effect. The complainant can then be compensated for any infringing products imported during this period by recovering the bond money through an ITC administered process. If the USTR disapproves the ITC's determination, the products are permitted to enter U.S. commerce. The USTR has disapproved an ITC determination one time since the President assigned this authority to the USTR in 2005.

[14] For the purposes of this report, "rescission" refers to the revocation, cancellation, or repeal of an exclusion order. In this instance, ITC has the authority to rescind an exclusion order if it determines that the conditions that required the exclusion order have changed such that a rescission is appropriate. 19 U.S.C. § 1337(k) and 19 C.F.R. § 210.76 (a)(b).

[15] 19 U.S.C. § 1337(d)(1).

[16] CBP national targeting groups develop targeting strategies for identifying shipments with products subject to exclusion orders.

[17] In fiscal year 2012, CBP launched Centers of Excellence and Expertise to provide a single point of contact for participating importers when processing their shipments. Each center provides support to importers within key industry sectors and consists of CBP staff at U.S. ports with related commodity expertise. As of November 2014, CBP officials said that 1 of the 10 centers—the Electronics Center—was fully established and participated in CBP's enforcement of exclusion orders. For more information on the centers, see app. III.

[18] Throughout this report, "complainant" refers to the party in an ITC investigation who initiated the investigation and whose intellectual property rights or domestic industry is protected by an exclusion order. "Respondent" refers to a party in an ITC investigation whose product or products are alleged to infringe the intellectual property rights of the corresponding complainant, or who has otherwise been proved to have committed unfair acts or methods of competition in violation of Section 337 (e.g., trade secret misappropriation).

[19] CBP's Automated Targeting System compares traveler, cargo, and conveyance information against law enforcement, intelligence, and other enforcement data to support CBP in identifying individuals and cargo that need additional review across the different means of transportation.

[20] In addition to its Automated Targeting System, CBP may also consult its Automated Commercial Environment, a system that processes information on shipments submitted by importers and exporters, enabling CBP to learn more about incoming shipments.

[21] CBP enforces laws for 40 other government agencies, such as the U.S. Fish and Wildlife Service, the U.S. Department of Agriculture, and the Centers for Disease Control and Prevention.

[22] IPR-NTAG officials said though they have initiated operations for other types of intellectual property enforcement, they had not initiated operations of this nature for exclusion order enforcement as of April 2014.

[23] According to an IPR Branch official, an ITC exclusion order generally allows an importer whose shipment has been excluded to request a warehouse entry or an application for foreign trade-zone admission from CBP. The official further explained that an importer can

also protest an exclusion by filing a protest with the director of the port where the exclusion occurred.

[24] 19 C.F.R. § 210.75(b)(6).

[25] According to CBP, if a shipment is seized pursuant to an ITC seizure and forfeiture order, the importer can file a petition for administrative relief pursuant to 19 U.S.C. § 1618 or, by filing a claim and cost bond, seek judicial review in accordance with 19 U.S.C. § 1608.

[26] Port officials may allow a shipment to enter the country and then take up to 30 days to determine whether the product is covered by an exclusion order. If CBP determines that the product is covered by an exclusion order after it has entered into U.S. commerce, CBP will demand redelivery of the shipment. See 19 C.F.R § 113.62(d).

[27] CBP developed this system in response to a recommendation in our 2008 report that CBP collect data on the number of exclusions (denials of entry), in total and per exclusion order. See GAO, Intellectual Property: Federal Enforcement Has Generally Increased, but Assessing Performance Could Strengthen Law Enforcement Efforts, GAO-08-157 (Washington, D.C.: Mar. 11, 2008). CBP officials said that they do not track the number of examinations that did not result in exclusions.

[28] GAO-08-157.

[29] Office of the Intellectual Property Enforcement Coordinator, Administration's White Paper on Intellectual Property Enforcement Legislative Recommendations (Washington, D.C.: March 2011).

[30] 19 C.F.R. Part 177. These regulations detail CBP's general processes to respond to an importer's request to obtain certainty in its import transaction about the admissibility of its product.

[31] CBP and ITC officials noted that ITC does not provide guidance to CBP on products that were not the subject of ITC's original Section 337 investigation.

[32] The 90-day time frame is set by 19 C.F.R. § 177.10.

[33] 19 C.F.R. § 177.12.

[34] Id.

[35] According to CBP officials, the approval of a certification is entirely at the discretion of CBP. CBP officials also noted that the acceptance of a certification for the purpose of entry does not establish any precedent as to CBP's acceptance of the certification for future shipments.

[36] According to CBP officials, a draft "notice of proposed rule-making" (notice) that would institute the inter partes process within its administrative rulings process has been completed. The notice explains the need for creating the inter partes procedures and proposes that a new subsection be added to existing regulations. The notice must be reviewed and cleared by CBP and approved by the Department of the Treasury. CBP will then give the public 60 days to submit comments on the notice. After the public comment period has closed, CBP must analyze the comments and respond to them and incorporate any changes to the proposed regulations. Once this process has been completed, the draft final rule must be reviewed and cleared again by CBP and approved by the Department of the Treasury prior to publication in the Federal Register. As of October 2014, the draft notice was with CBP's Trade and Commercial Regulations Branch, Regulations and Rulings Directorate, which is responsible for shepherding the document through the internal and interagency review process.

[37] For the purposes of this report, "rescission" refers to the revocation, cancellation, or repeal of an exclusion order. In this instance, ITC has the authority to rescind exclusion orders if it determines that the conditions that required the exclusion order have changed such that a rescission is appropriate. 19 U.S.C. § 1337(k) and 19 C.F.R. § 210.76 (a)(b).

[38] GAO-08-157.

[39] 19 C.F.R. § 12.39.

[40] Officials told us that the CBP intranet, which was developed in 2004, is accessible to all CBP staff in headquarters, field offices, and ports.

[41] OMB Circular No. A-123 and GAO/AIMD-00-21.3.1. Internal control, in the broadest sense, includes the plan of organization, methods, and procedures adopted by management to meet its goals.

[42] ITC issued these 17 exclusion orders between 1990 and 1997.

[43] 19 C.F.R. § 210.76(a).

[44] Based on CBP's letter to the ITC, the ITC published a notice in the Federal Register seeking public comments as to whether the 6 exclusion orders should be rescinded in whole or in part based on changed conditions of fact or law or the public interest pursuant to 19 C.F.R. § 210.76. See 79 Fed. Reg. 64214 (Oct. 28, 2014). Written submissions are due on December 22, 2014, and reply submissions on January 15, 2015.

[45] While CBP does not track local targeting efforts, CBP records excluded shipments and the national targeting methods used to identify them. Our analysis of CBP's data on exclusions related to the 27 exclusion orders without trade alerts posted on the intranet found two exclusions that were the result of local targeting. These two exclusions occurred in fiscal year 2010 and were related to 1 of the 27 orders with no trade alert on the intranet.

[46] IPR Branch officials said that 2 of the 27 exclusion orders were older trademark-based orders and seizures were made because of trademark violations.

[47] GAO-08-157.

[48] OMB Circular No. A-123 and GAO/AIMD-00-21.3.1.

[49] In our 2008 report, we found that it took CBP more than 60 days to post trade alerts for 14 of the 18 exclusion orders for which it could provide such data. See GAO-08-157.

[50] OMB Circular No. A-123.

End Notes for Appendix

[1] The litigation involves CBP's enforcement efforts pertaining to an exclusion order issued by ITC, finding a violation of Section 337 because certain Motorola products had infringed Microsoft's patent rights. Microsoft Corporation v. Dep't of Homeland Sec. et al, 1:13-cv 01063-RWR (D.D.C. July 12, 2013).

[2] We used data starting from September 16, 2010, because CBP started tracking exclusions in its exclusion order notification and tracking system on this date.

[3] 19 C.F.R. § 12.39.

[4] Office of Management and Budget, Management's Responsibility for Internal Control, OMB Circular No. A-123 (Washington, D.C.: Dec. 21, 2004) and GAO, Standards for Internal Control in the Federal Government, GAO/AIMD-00-21.3.1 (Washington, D.C.: November 1999)

[5] 19 C.F.R. § 177.10 Part 177.

INDEX

C

D

E

F

N

O

P

Q

R

S

T

U

V

W